SPIRIT VS. FLESH

A CONSTANT BATTLE

Dr. Pamala Wilson

WESTBOW
PRESS®
A DIVISION OF THOMAS NELSON
& ZONDERVAN

WestBow Press books may be ordered through booksellers or by contacting:

WestBow Press
A Division of Thomas Nelson & Zondervan
1663 Liberty Drive
Bloomington, IN 47403
www.westbowpress.com
1 (866) 928-1240

ISBN: 978-1-9736-5850-4 (sc)
ISBN: 978-1-9736-5851-1 (hc)
ISBN: 978-1-9736-5849-8 (e)

Library of Congress Control Number: 2019904158

Print information available on the last page.

WestBow Press rev. date: 07/08/2019

DEDICATION

I want to dedicate this book to my faithful daughter, Morgan, who knows my calling and purpose for life and loves me for whom and what God has called me to be. She supports me in all I do and always has an encouraging word or smile for me as I move forward in my journey fulfilling the purpose I was created for.

Morgan, the love I have for you is the closest thing to my understanding of our eternal father's unconditional love for us. I always told you that all I wanted was for you and your life to bring God glory. You are living out my prayer. Thank you for being in my life. Thank you for ministering to me. You are such a blessing and a gift from above.

Cole, my son-in-law, you are such a blessing to Morgan and me. Thank you for being the husband for my daughter that I had prayed for all these years but just didn't know your name. I am so proud of the young man you are becoming as you seek God and his perfect will for you and your family. You are a great addition to our family.

I also want to thank my brother Chuck and his family: Cady, Blake, Kaylin, Daven, and Allie, who are always there for me offering me encouragement in the ongoing endeavors that God has entrusted to me.

Lastly, I want to thank all of my work friends who have been there with me through the writing process of this book and have always offered encouragement.

I want to thank Dr. Tim Fagan, who held me accountable to finish my book by always asking me how the book was coming along and when I would be finished.

CONTENTS

PART 3   WINNING THE BATTLE

PREFACE

T his is my first attempt at writing a book. I never dreamed I would be called to write something because English and literature were my least favorite subjects and were therefore, the culprits of my grade point average being lower than it could have been. Thank God, he doesn't look for ability but availability. Priscilla Shirer said, "God doesn't call the equipped; he equips the called!"[1] It is when we are called and available that he makes us able. It is in our weaknesses that his strength is most revealed.

When God Makes Us Equipped and Able, We Not Only Go to Church, We Are the Church.

I wanted to write *Spirit Vs Flesh* because of my battle with this for the first forty years of my life. I was finally victorious at the lowest time in my life because of Jesus Christ. You see, sometimes that is the very place where God gets our attention—at the bottom or lowest point of our lives and the only direction to look is up.

My story begins like this. I grew up in Arkansas in a middle-class family with one older sister and one younger brother. My father was a civil engineer, and my mother was a homemaker. As we got older, she started working as a teacher's aide. My family was not a Christian one. We would go to church only on rare occasions, and mostly without my dad.

I was the baby girl of the family and the apple of my dad's eye. I was the one who would run out and jump into his arms when he arrived home from work. I was his shadow. Needless to say, I idolized my daddy.

As I got older, I realized that my daddy was an alcoholic and abused my mother physically, verbally, and emotionally. I remember many times as a child, standing between my dad's next swing and my mother. He would stop when one of us children got in the way, because he wouldn't hit us.

This caused great pain in our family and an insecure environment for me to grow up and learn. I began to think that if my dad could hurt my mom, then any man could hurt me. So, I constructed invisible walls of protection around my heart early in my life.

When I was a junior in high school, I met my first love, who was a football player. I treated him badly due to my experience with relationships. I had fallen for him because of the attention he would give me. I eventually lost my virginity to him and also my heart, even though my actions were mean and harsh toward him. We dated throughout high school and then went to separate colleges.

During our first year of college, we would come home most weekends to see each other. I was so in love with him, or so I thought in my youthful mind. During that first year of college, we broke up, and I was heartbroken. I had never felt pain like that before. It was a gut-wrenching pain of betrayal and rejection that you wouldn't wish on your worst enemy.

After that, I secured the invisible walls of protection around my heart against men. I felt I always had to have a boyfriend, for security and worth, but would never let him get close to me. I don't mean physically, but emotionally. I numbed myself, towards men so I wouldn't get hurt, like my daddy and first love had hurt me. However, I would give myself away physically on the second or third date—sometimes on the first—to gain their acceptance. I began to view myself as having nothing of value or self-worth.

I kept searching for the Prince Charming that I was supposed to meet, fall madly in love, get married, and live happily ever after—like Snow White and Cinderella. After all, isn't that what life is all about? Each time I entered a relationship and the newness and euphoria ended, I just discounted it to not being my Prince Charming.

When I couldn't find that fulfillment in men, I started drinking alcohol more and more. During this time, I worked on getting a graduate degree because I thought money would help me attain happiness. I went into the nursing profession that would make the most money. I thought that the money might fulfill me, because men and alcohol weren't doing the trick.

I graduated with an advanced degree and started making great money.

Wow! I thought if I could buy almost everything I wanted, that would fulfill me. But yet again, I came up empty and void inside.

The things the world said would bring happiness just made me burdened and tired, trying to relentlessly pursue something that would satisfy. I kept consuming alcohol almost daily and I did some other drugs, occasionally. I was trying to numb my pain and hurt, lessen my burdens, and most of all, fill the void deep in my heart that had not been filled with the things of the world.

At the age of forty, I found myself in southern California. I moved because of my relationship with another man. By this time in my life, I had sexually been with over thirty men and one female. I had had six plastic surgeries, three abortions, and I was an alcoholic, smoker, and drug abuser. Quite a track record—or not!

My boyfriend had a friend who asked us to go to Saddleback Church with him and his wife, so we went and really liked it. The pastor, Rick Warren, had written a book called *The Purpose Driven Life*.

After going to church, I picked up a few copies of the book and started reading it in June of 2004. It made sense to me, was practical and understandable, and had answers that I had been searching for all my life. I remember my daddy saying so many times, "There has got to be more to life than this," but not knowing the answer.

In reading this book, I found what I had been looking for all along. I wasn't an accident. I had been created for a purpose. My heart began to change. I was not able to handle the burden of my sins. I hated who I had become but couldn't do anything about it myself.

On a Sunday morning in July of 2004 after a night of pornography, alcohol, smoking, and sex with my boyfriend, I couldn't take it anymore. I hated who I had become, kept messing up, and couldn't do anything about it in my own strength and power. I got on my knees and asked Jesus Christ into my heart, to forgive me of all of my sins, and to be the boss and Savior of my life.

Wow! I got up and felt something I had never felt before. I felt clean, light, forgiven, and loved in a way I had been looking for my whole life. He, Jesus Christ, had been what I was missing all along, and he had been there waiting for me to come to him.

I was a new person in Christ and didn't have the same desires anymore.

I was immediately delivered from my slavery of sin. I didn't want to drink alcohol, smoke, or have sex with my boyfriend. No! I was hungry for the things of the Spirit. I was immediately free from myself. I started going to church and reading my Bible. I finished *The Purpose Driven Life* and was on fire for Christ.

I still struggle and have trials but also have Jesus Christ in me and with me to help me through them all. Beth Moore said, "Few truly know the unfailing love of God like the captive set free."[2] I have experienced this truth and couldn't agree more with this statement.

After finding Jesus, I chose, after sometime and many poor choices, to terminate the most emotionally exhausting relationship I had ever been involved. So, I left him and moved from California back home to Oklahoma.

I know God was in this move for many reasons. God works when something is his perfect will for your life. I got a great job, bought a home right across the street from my brother, and put my daughter into a Christian school. This is also *so* God. My daughter was into horseback riding, and her trainer at that time had her son and daughter-in-law training in Owasso, Oklahoma. Now that is no coincidence, but it is God.

My daughter and I flew to Oklahoma on July 4th, 2006, and while we were landing, fireworks were going off all around us. The Holy Spirit spoke to me deeply and said, "You are free."

I am presently living in Oklahoma where I moved to be closer to family. I joined the First Baptist Church in Owasso, Oklahoma, and started feeding my spirit daily. I learned the word of God—the Bible—through intense reading, studying, journaling, praying, and fellowshipping with other Christians.

After about two years, I started feeling the Spirit prompting me to serve in the student ministry. I served as a small group leader on Wednesday nights and then went to a summer camp with the youth. I then felt led by the Spirit to start teaching Sunday school to young teen girls. I have been teaching for over ten years. They are my passion, and I know that I am fulfilling the purpose I was created for.

When you are doing and fulfilling your God-given purpose, there is a euphoria and sense of satisfaction that I had never experienced. And, there wasn't a hangover, guilt, or regret.

The Bible says:

1. "And we know that in all things God works for the good of those who love him, who have been called according to his purpose." [3]
2. God makes "beauty instead of ashes."[4] God allowed me to use my mistakes in life and share them with the girls whom he had placed in my sphere of influence.
3. "For we are God's handiwork, created in Christ Jesus to do good works, which God prepared in advance for us to do."[5]

If I can keep one of these girls from going down the wrong path or making a wrong choice by sharing my personal and painful experiences, my life will have served a great purpose. When doing this in my life, God takes my ashes (mistakes) and makes them beautiful.

I would like you to watch my story on YouTube before going any further in the book. It will help you to see and to hear what Jesus did inside me when I accepted him as my personal Lord and Savior. Go to www.youtube.com and type in "Pam Wilson's story" in the search bar.

NOTES

1   Priscilla Shirer, *And We Are Changed: Encounters With a Transforming God* (Chicago: Moody Publishers, 2003), 148.
2   Beth Moore, *Breaking Free: Making Liberty in Christ a Reality in Life* (Nashville: B & H Publishing Group, 2000), 202.
3   Romans 8:28 *New International Version* (NIV)
4   Isaiah 61:3 NIV
5   Ephesians 2:10 NIV

INTRODUCTION

There is a constant battle that most of us are not even aware is occurring in our lives. For the first forty years of my life, I lived in defeat because I did not realize that I was in that battle. The most dangerous part of being in a battle is not realizing that you are in one.

The battle that I am referring to is between the Holy Spirit and our flesh.

For the flesh desires what is contrary to the Spirit, and the Spirit what is contrary to the flesh. They are in conflict with each other, so that you are not to do whatever you want.[1]

We need to ask God to crucify our natural, sinful, fleshly desires and to empower us in the Spirit.

So I say, walk by the Spirit, and you will not gratify the desires of the flesh.[2]

You see, believers, **it is Imperative to Feed our Spirits and to Starve our Flesh so that our Spirits and not our Flesh are Empowered. The one you Feed is the one that is Empowered.** When we feed our spirits through quiet time with God, Bible study, journaling, praying, serving, fellowship, meditating, and applying God's truths to our lives, we lose our appetite for the fleshly desires and desire what is pleasing to the Holy Spirit.

The flesh is self-seeking and our default mode. Our natural sinful nature is a result of humankind's fall to sin. The Bible says,

Those who live according to the flesh have their minds set on what the flesh desires; but those who live in accordance with the Spirit have their minds set on what the Spirit desires. The mind governed by the flesh is death, but the mind governed by the Spirit is life and peace. The mind governed by the flesh is hostile to God; it does not submit to God's law, nor can it do so. Those who are in the realm of the flesh cannot please God.

You, however, are not in the realm of the flesh but are in the realm of the Spirit, if indeed the Spirit of God lives in you. And if anyone does not have the Spirit of Christ, they do not belong to Christ."[3]

You *can* lose the battle and default back to your fleshly desires if you don't develop a relationship with God through his Holy Spirit. Andy Stanley said, "Rules without a relationship lead to rebellion."[4]

I am burdened by the fact that more Christians live to gratify their flesh than doing what is pleasing to the Spirit—thus my stimulus to write this book. Our burdens can be used by the Holy Spirit to stimulate change in our and other people's lives. **It is the Burdens in our Heart that Become the Passions of our Heart.** Hopefully, through the message in this book, other Christians will wake up to the battle we face while living here on earth. I pray they will live again in victory that is being empowered by the Spirit, instead of in defeat that is being empowered by the flesh.

Believers, please hear this. Jesus came for *two* reasons. First, he came so that we could live eternally in God's presence in heaven. Second, he came to free us from our slavery to sin while here on the earth. After our spiritual birth, we are assured of our adoption as children of God, our belonging to the body of believers, and that our eternal forwarding address will change from hell to heaven.

However, we don't take advantage of the second reason God sent his Son. Jesus Christ also died to free us from our slavery to sin. We don't have to lose our battle to the flesh. We can live in victory, not through our own strength but through the power of the Holy Spirit, who comes to live in each one of us as believers in Jesus Christ. Those of us who do not have the Spirit of God living in us are not Christians at all.

Now that you understand why we are losing the battle, you will also understand why we don't look any different than the lost people of this world. We are still living empowered by the flesh and not the Spirit. We are called hypocrites because we live like we are not only in the world but of the world. We are called to be in the world and not of the world.

If you belonged to the world it would love you as its own. As it is, you do not belong to the world, but I have chosen you out of the world. That is why the world hates you.[5]

I pray that the message I have been called to share will wake all Christians up to live each day empowered by the Spirit and not the flesh. I have great hope and faith that we will start living, not just acknowledging God with our mouths, but also in the way we live our lives. **If You are not Walking it, don't Talk it.** That will do less harm to the kingdom of God. I also pray that through Spirit-filled, daily living, we can become more like Christ. As we become more like Christ, we can bring others to know him as well. *We* can make an invisible God more visible through us as the vessel. After all, that is why believers have been left here on earth, isn't it?

NOTES

1   Galatians 5:17 NIV
2   Galatians 5:16 NIV
3   Romans 8:5–9 NIV
4   Andy Stanley, "Preaching The Grace of The Law," Sermon Central, November 29, 2010, https://www.sermoncentral.com/pastors-preaching-articles/ andy-stanley-preaching-the-grace-of-the-law-763?ref=PreachingArticleDetails.
5   John 15:19 NIV

PART ONE

THE CHOICE

CHAPTER 1

The Fall

When God created humankind, he intended to have a *complete* relationship with us. Adam and Eve lived in the garden of Eden where they enjoyed complete relationships with God. But because Adam and Eve sinned against the will of God when they ate the fruit from the forbidden tree of the knowledge of good and evil, they were thrown out of the garden of Eden and separated from God on earth. This is referred to as the fall of humankind. They fell from God's presence.

The fall of humankind refers to the separation of humankind from God due to the presence of sin. We are all descendants of Adam and Eve, and since they sinned against God, we were also born as sinners into this world. We inherit our sinful nature from Adam and Eve and so does all humankind.

Making Mistakes Is Not the Problem, Not Learning From Them Is.

You see, God is perfect, and we are not. God cannot be in the presence of sin. So, when we were born as sinners, we were separated from him. But nothing can separate us from God's *love*.

Neither height nor depth, nor anything else in all creation, will be able to separate us from the love of God that is in Christ Jesus our Lord.[1]

Nothing Separates us from God's Love, but Sin Separates us from God. God's original design was for us to be in his complete presence.

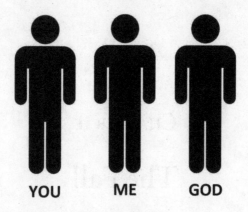

God's original design

Our sin is what separates us from God.

Sin separates us from God.

For all have sinned and fall short of the glory of God.[2]

The consequences of our sin are physical and spiritual death. But God has a plan so that we can come back into his presence. God loves you, and he created you to have a relationship with him.

NOTES

1   Romans 8:39 NIV
2   Romans 3:23 NIV

CHAPTER 2

God's Redemptive Plan

G od had a plan for humankind to be able to come back into his presence. He searched for a way back, if you will, into the garden of Eden. But since God is perfect and cannot be in the presence of sin, he established a plan where we can be forgiven of our sins. He created a plan to make us clean, pure, and forgiven.

For the wages of sin is death, but the gift of God is eternal life in Christ Jesus our Lord.[1]

But God demonstrated his own love for us in this: while we were still sinners, Christ died for us.[2]

Jesus Christ took our sins to the cross on our behalf and paid our debt in full by dying a criminal's death on the cross. He took our punishment for us.

But he was pierced for our transgressions, he was crushed for our iniquities; the punishment that brought us peace was on him, and by his wounds we are healed.[3]

God gave us the option of receiving a gift through his Son, Jesus Christ. If we accept Jesus Christ, we are forgiven of our sins because of what Jesus did for us on the cross.

If you declare with your mouth, "Jesus is Lord," and believe in your heart that God raised him from the dead, you will be saved.[4]

The Bible also says, "Everyone who calls on the name of the Lord will be saved.[5]

Because of Jesus's ultimate sacrifice, we can be in his presence again when we have received his forgiveness.

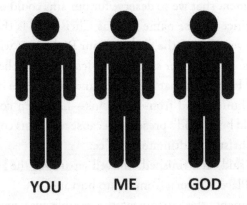

We are forgiven of our sins and can enter God's presence again.

Because of Christ's sacrifice, we now have peace with God. **We Can be in God's Presence, not Because we are Sinless but Because we are Forgiven.**

Therefore, since we have been justified through faith, we have peace with God through our Lord Jesus Christ.[6]

Also, we will not be condemned for our sins.

Therefore, there is now no condemnation for those who are in Christ Jesus.[7]

Our sins are paid in full. This does not mean that we won't be punished or face the consequences of our bad choices, which lead to sin, but we won't be denied eternal life in heaven with God or the forgiveness he so freely offers.

He has removed our sins as far from us as the east is from the west.[8]

God created us in love. He was willing to do whatever it took to bring us back to him. His sacrificial, unfailing love for us and his desire for fellowship with us caused him to send and sacrifice his greatest treasure: his one and only precious Son, whose name is Jesus Christ.

For God so loved the world that he gave his only Son, so that everyone who believes in him will not perish but have eternal life.[9]

So, God's plan was to send a Savior who was perfect, was without sin, and could take our punishment for us.

And being found in appearance as a man, he humbled himself by becoming obedient to death—even death on a cross![10]

The punishment that we so deserve for our sins could only be forgiven by a sinless sacrifice, whose name is Jesus Christ. He is the one and only Son of God. He was God in the flesh and our Redeemer, who came to save us and to pay the price for our sins. When Jesus was on the cross, he said, "It is finished."[11] He meant that the reason and purpose he had come to the world—to save humankind from their sins—had been completed. Now humankind could be in God's presence because their sins could be forgiven through Jesus Christ, the ultimate sacrifice.

When Jesus said, "It is finished," the veil separating the Holy Place from the Most Holy Place was torn from top to bottom.

At that moment, the curtain of the temple was torn from top to bottom.[12]

This signified that the separation between humankind and God was no longer a problem.

We all now have equal access to God because of what Jesus did on the cross. Billy Graham said, "The ground is level at the foot of the cross."[13]

Because Jesus paid the penalty for our sins, through his forgiveness we can be in the presence of God again. Hallelujah!

Jesus told him, I am the way, the truth, and the life. No one can come through the father except through me.[14]

Through Jesus, we can be forgiven and enter into God's presence again.

When you give your life to Jesus Christ, you will be saved from earthly and eternal separation from God. The ABCs of salvation are:

A. Admit

Admit that you have sinned, ask God to forgive your sins, and be willing to turn from your sins. You must repent—turn from your sins and walk the other way. **Our Forgiveness is not Limited by our Amount or Type of Sin but by the Extent to Which we are Willing to Repent.**

B. Believe

Believe that Jesus is God's Son who died in your place, rose from the dead, and sits on the throne at the right hand of God.

C. Call

Call on the Lord, confess your sins, and commit your life to him.

By doing the steps above, we have secured our forwarding eternal address from hell to heaven. If you did this for the first time, congratulations! You have made the most important decision of your life. The angels in heaven are celebrating that you will be with them for eternity.

We Are Born Physically Into Sin, But We Are Reborn Spiritually Into Freedom From Sin.

But it doesn't stop here. This is as far as many Christians get, and that is where the problem lies. Salvation alone does not make you fulfilled and satisfied with your life here on earth. Satisfaction and true fulfillment come when we have an intimate relationship with Jesus Christ and are fulfilling our God-given purpose.

If we didn't have a reason to stay on earth after being saved, we would just go right to heaven (a.k.a. paradise). We are left here for two main purposes. First, we are here to become more like Christ and to be sanctified—to grow up in our faith—through developing a relationship with him by spending time in Bible study, prayer, journaling, meditation on his Word, application, fellowship, and service. As you spend time with him, you get to know him more and become more like him by applying what you have learned to your life. We are to grow up in our spirituality and not stay as infants in our faith.

Like newborn babies, crave pure spiritual milk, so that by it you may grow up in your salvation.[15]

Second, we are called to expand his kingdom by bringing others to Christ. As we become more like Christ, we become better representatives for him. He becomes more visible in us to the lost people of the world who are desperately seeking to find what we have.

So, let's read the next chapter to understand the battle that Christians face continually. By understanding that this battle exists, we can live victoriously full and abundant lives and fulfill our earthly purpose.

The thief comes to steal and kill and destroy; I have come that they might have life, and have it to the full.[16]

NOTES

1   Romans 6:23 NIV
2   Romans 5:8 NIV
3   Isaiah 53:5 NIV
4   Romans 10:9 NIV
5   Romans 10:13 NIV
6   Romans 5:1 NIV
7   Romans 8:1 NIV
8   Psalm 103:12 *New Living Translation* (NLT)
9   John 3:16 NIV
10 Philippians 2:8 NIV
11 John 19:30 NIV
12 Matthew 27:51 NIV
13 Dr. J.C. Pollock, *The Billy Graham Story* (Grand Rapids: Zondervan, 2003), 113.
14 John 14:6 NIV
15 1 Peter 2:2 NIV
16 John 10:10 NIV

CHAPTER 3

The Constant Battle

After accepting Jesus Christ as our Lord and Savior, we are now saved not only from an eternal separation, but an earthly separation from God. Our fulfillment and satisfaction in our earthly lives come not only from our salvation and eternal destination, but also from an intimate relationship with God through his Son, Jesus Christ.

We are still sinful-natured humans who need to continually crucify ourselves and our natural sinful, fleshly desires and empower ourselves through the Holy Spirit. If we don't, we will automatically default to the flesh. We will live in the flesh, not the Spirit, and be just like the world. When we live just like the world, we will provide no light in the darkness and negate the purpose we have been left to fulfill on the earth after our salvation. Otherwise, when we are saved we would immediately go home.

We Work for God Because We Are Saved, Not To Be Saved.

There is a battle between our flesh and our spirit.

So I say, let the Holy Spirit guide your lives. Then you won't be doing what your sinful nature craves. The sinful nature wants to do evil, which is just the opposite of what the Spirit wants. And the Spirit gives us desires that are the opposite of what the sinful nature desires. These two forces are constantly fighting each other, so you are not free to carry out your good intentions. But when you are directed by the Spirit, you are not under obligation to the law of Moses.[1]

This verse also speaks of the battle between the Spirit and the flesh:

"Dear friends, I warn you as 'temporary residents and foreigners' to keep away from worldly desires that wage war against your very souls."[2] The Bible also speaks of the battle here: "What is causing the quarrels and fights among you? Isn't it the whole army of evil desires at war within you?"[3]

So, believers, do you see that there is a battle of spirit and flesh going on constantly in your lives? Jesus spoke of the choice to live in the flesh or the spirit when he said, "Whoever wants to be my disciple must deny themselves and take up their cross and follow me."[4]

So let's look at the cross and the illustration I have given.

Through Jesus, we can be forgiven and enter into God's presence again.

Now, let me ask you a question. Are you going to live each day separated from God by sin or are you going to live each day in the presence of God through his Son, Jesus Christ?

Is it going to be here?

Separated from God by sin

Or is it going to be here?

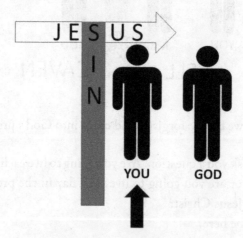

Present with God by forgiveness of sin

Let's now look at each side of the cross and see what the results of our choices will be.

Results of our choices to live in sin or to be forgiven of sin

Now, you can see the results of our choice, to live either controlled by the Spirit through Jesus Christ or by the flesh through rebellion—the default. The consequences of our choice are noted above. We will discuss each one in detail in the chapters that follow. As you go through each fleshly or spiritual attribute, I suggest that you pick one attribute a day and reflect on the chapter that is associated with it before moving on to the next.

We all learn in one of two ways: through wisdom when we understand the lesson before the action, or through knowledge when we understand the lesson after the action. Wisdom is a far greater way to learn the lessons of life and to avoid the painful experiences and consequences of poor decisions. Strive to learn by wisdom and not by knowledge.

NOTES

1   Galatians 5: 16–18 NLT
2   1 Peter 2:11 NLT
3   James 4:1 NLT
4   Matthew 16:24 NIV

PART TWO

RESULTS OF YOUR CHOICES

CHAPTER 4

Love Vs Hate

The first result of our choice to live in either the Spirit or the flesh is love or hate. Are you going to live each day empowered by the Spirit to love, or be enslaved by the flesh to hate?

The world teaches us that love is a feeling or emotion. Love can most definitely produce feelings and emotions, but it is much more than that.

You see, the world has got it all wrong. Since when is love a feeling or a sexual attraction? If that is what love is, then are we no longer in love when we stop feeling love for or are not sexually attracted to another? We can tell that is what the world believes due to the number of divorces and infidelity today. The sad part is that Christians' divorce rates are not much different from the worlds. I have contributed to that statistic. No wonder we are called hypocrites. The truth is we are hypocrites if we are no different than the world.

Love is not a feeling at all. It is an action. God proved his love for us by his ultimate action: While we were still sinners, he laid down his only Son's life for us.

Love Can Only Be Known by the Actions It Produces.

"Dear children, let us not love with words or speech but with actions and in truth. This is how we know that we belong to the truth and how we set our hearts at rest in his presence."[1] The Bible also says, "And this is love: that we walk in obedience to his commands. As you have heard from the beginning, his command is that you walk in love."[2] Our obedience to God's commands is the ultimate action that proves that we are children of God.

As humans, we are wired to want this euphoric, intimate attraction that will never fade or go away. When this feeling goes away, we get another new relationship that gives us the same euphoric feeling, and on and on.

I know firsthand because I was on that same road. I have had over thirty relationships in my life, including two marriages. Each time the newness wore off, I would start looking for a new victim. My thought process was that I just had not met Mr. Right. I was brought up like a lot of little girls to believe the fantasy that there is a Prince Charming, and when you meet him and get married, you will live happily ever after. Wow! It sounds great until you grow up and realize that we have been betrayed by the lies of the world.

We were Created with a Need for Unfailing Love, and We will Go to Great Measures Relentlessly Pursuing that Kind of Love.

Just As an Inventor Knows Best His Invention, So Too Does the Creator Know Best His Creation.

What a person desires is unfailing love.[3]
You see, our Creator did this for a reason.

He Created Us With a Void Or Deep Need That Only He, the Creator, Could Fill.

When we get tired of looking in the world for the kind of love that doesn't exist, we will look toward him and realize that *he*, our Creator, is all we have ever needed. The Lord said, "I have loved you with an everlasting love; I have drawn you with unfailing kindness."[4] He is the ultimate and only source of everlasting, unfailing love. His unfailing love endures forever.

The Bible says,

Love is patient, love is kind. It does not envy, it does not boast, it is not proud. It does not dishonor others, it is not self-seeking, it is not easily angered, it keeps no record of wrongs. Love does not delight in evil but rejoices with the truth. It always protects, always trusts, always hopes, always perseveres.[5]

And now there are three things that remain: faith, hope and love. But the greatest of these is love.[6]

The best way to comprehend God's love for each of us is to think about the child we brought into the world. If you are a parent, you understand the unconditional love you have for your child. This is what the Bible says God's love for us is like, but so much more.

And I pray that you, being rooted and established in love, may have power, together with all the Lord's holy people, to grasp how wide and long and high and deep is the love of Christ, and to know this love that surpasses knowledge that you may be filled to the measure of all the fullness of God.[7]

But even the kind of love we humans have for our children does not compare to God's love for each of us. We humanize God when we try to understand his love for us. God is infinite and we are finite.

We Are Humans With a Finite Mind That Continually Tries to Comprehend an Infinite God.

You see, God can't stop loving you no matter what you do. The Bible says, "And so we know and rely on the love God has for us. God is love. Whoever lives in love lives in God, and God in them."[8] God not only loves, he is love. It is who he is. So, if he stopped loving, he would stop being. God is the noun and not the verb for love. God is love.

When Jesus spoke during his ministry here on earth, he gave us the two greatest commandments to live by regarding love. The Bible says, "Love the Lord your God with all your heart and with all your soul and with all your mind. This is the first and greatest commandment. And the second is like it: 'Love your neighbor as yourself.' All the Law and the Prophets hang on these two commandments."[9] So if we love God first and others as ourselves, we will be obeying all the other commands.

We Call the Kind of Love We Have In Christ Selfless and Not Selfish Love.

Now, here is where it gets hard. It is easy to love people who are loving, but what about our enemies? We are to love them also, and that is where our love is really tested. The Bible says,

21

But if you are willing to listen I say, love your enemies. Do good to those who hate you. Pray for the happiness of those who curse you. Pray for those who hurt you. If someone slaps you on the cheek, turn the other cheek. If someone demands your coat, offer your shirt also. Give what you have to anyone who asks you for it; and when things are taken away from you, don't try to get them back. Do for others as you would like them to do for you.

Do you think you deserve credit merely for loving those who love you? Even sinners do that! And if you do good only to those who do good to you, is that so wonderful? Even sinners do that much! And if you lend money only to those who can repay you, what good is that? Even sinners will lend to their kind for a full return.

Love your enemies! Do good to them! Lend to them! And don't be concerned that they might not repay. Then your reward from heaven will be very great, and you will truly be acting as children of the Most High, for he is kind to the unthankful and to those who are wicked. You must be compassionate, just as your Father is compassionate.[10]

When We Can Truly Love Our Enemies, We Show Who We Are and Whose We Are.

When we pass this test, we make an invisible God visible through his Holy Spirit, who empowers us to love others, especially the unworthy. Our eternal reward from heaven will be great, and we will be adding to our inheritance. We can't do this in our own strength, but he gives us the divine inheritance of his Holy Spirit, who can do this through us as available vessels.

When We Are Available, He Makes Us Able.

Now let's talk a little more about the ability to love. It is not in our natural human sinful nature to love anyone but ourselves. This is a selfish, not selfless love.

In Our Flesh, We Are Only Able to Worship the Earthly Trinity of Me, Myself, and I, Not the Holy Trinity of the Father, Son, and Holy Spirit.

Do not love this world nor the things it offers you, for when you love the world, you do not have the love of the Father in you. For the world offers only a craving for physical pleasure, a craving for everything we see, and pride in our achievements and possessions. These are not from the Father, but are from this world. And this world is fading away, along with everything that people crave. But anyone who does what pleases God will live forever.[11]

So the only way to love is through the power that is given to us from the Holy Spirit. Love is a fruit of the spirit.

But when the Holy Spirit controls our lives he will produce this kind of fruit in us: love, joy, peace, patience, kindness, goodness, faithfulness, gentleness and self-control.[12]

When are we able to produce the fruit that the Holy Spirit gives us? We produce fruit when we provide our spirit with nourishment from reading, studying, praying, journaling, meditating, serving, and most importantly, obeying and applying God's Word to our lives. When we feed and nourish our spirits, our spirits will be empowered to love.

When we don't feed our spirits, the flesh will be empowered to hate. When we don't live in the Spirit, our automatic human default setting is the opposite of the Holy Spirit's attributes. Again, the one that wins is the one that is fed. Which one are you feeding? Your appetite, cravings, and diet have earthly and eternal consequences.

NOTES

1   1 John 3:18 and 19 NIV
2   2 John 1:6 NIV
3   Proverbs 19:22 NIV
4   Jeremiah 31:3 NIV
5   1 Corinthians 13:4–7 NIV
6   1 Corinthians 13:13 NIV
7   Ephesians 3:17–19 NIV
8   1 John 4:16 NIV
9   Matthew 22:37–40 NIV
10 Luke 6:27–36 NLT
11 1 John 2:15–17 NLT
12 Galatians 5:22 *The Living Bible* (TLB)

CHAPTER 5

Joy Vs Sorrow

The next result of our choice to live in the Spirit or in the flesh is joy or sorrow. Are you going to live each day empowered by the Spirit to have joy or to be enslaved by the flesh to have sorrow?

Joy and happiness are used interchangeably, but there are some discrete differences between the two words. Joy is a constant internal attribute that comes from the Holy Spirit that non-believers can't comprehend or experience. **Happiness is a Feeling or Emotion Dependent on External Circumstances Rather than an Internal Quality.**

The joy Christians have is an internal attribute that is not based on external circumstances, because it is a fruit of the Holy Spirit that is internally present. One of my Christian mentors called it a "settled joy." I think of "settled" as a settling of our souls through Jesus Christ from the relentless pursuit of fulfillment. If you are depending on your external circumstances to bring you joy, you will live much of your life in sorrow.

Now let's look at what the Bible says about joy. Nehemiah said, "The joy of the Lord is your strength!"[1] Joy for believers is their strength. It gives us the strength to get through each day and is a constant internal reminder of our spiritual inheritance as children of God.

In Psalms, we read, "You will show me the way of life, granting me the joy of your presence and the pleasures of living with you forever."[2] In his presence, there is great joy. In his absence, there is great sorrow. We were created to be in the complete presence of God, as we discussed earlier. When we are not in his presence, we will not have his complete joy.

The above verse also says that God will show us the way of life. On my own, I don't know the way of life. When I have tried to be in the driver's seat of my life, I have made a huge mess of things. If he is showing me the way, then I will experience his presence and the joy and pleasure of living with him now and forever in heaven. Not only can we experience joy on earth, but eternal joy as well. Sounds like a deal to me!

David was pleading to God in this verse: "Restore to me the joy of your salvation, and make me willing to obey you."[3] David, who had committed adultery with Bathsheba, arranged for the killing of her husband in an attempt to cover up the sin, and was separated from God because of it.

God wants us to be close to him and to experience the complete, fulfilling, and joyful life that we can have in his presence. But if we are in an unrepentant sin pattern, we can't be in the presence of God. We lose that close, intimate relationship and experience a distance and separation between us and God. If we confess our sins, we can be back in his presence and enjoy the completeness that comes only from closeness to him. You might have to suffer some earthly consequences for your sins, but you can do it while being close to him and not all alone. God will return the joy of a relationship with him to us if we are not in a repetitive pattern of unconfessed sin.

Another way for us to have the joy of the Lord is revealed in this verse: "Light shines on the godly, and joy to those who are right."[4] We can have joy if we do what is right. If we do what is right, we live according to what is pleasing to God. If we please God, we will experience a close, intimate relationship that brings the unspeakable joy that comes only from being in his presence.

The Bible also speaks of righteousness and joy in this verse: "The prospect of the righteous is joy, but the hopes of the wicked come to nothing."[5] So righteousness and joy go hand in hand.

This verse in Isaiah also speaks of joy: "Those who have been ransomed by the LORD will return. They will enter Jerusalem singing, crowned with everlasting joy. Sorrow and mourning will disappear, and they will be filled with joy and gladness."[6] The Bible calls this the "Highway of Holiness."[7] Evil people will not travel this highway, only godly people. This highway, found only by following God, is lit, straight, full of purpose, and leads us home. Not only does he point the way, he travels with us. When we reach home, we will experience no more sorrow, but a joy that we cannot comprehend in our flesh.

Everlasting joy is found in this verse: "Instead of shame and dishonor, you shall have a double portion of prosperity and everlasting joy."[8] Wow! Sign me up for a *double* portion of prosperity and everlasting joy. This is something that the world would do almost anything for. However, it can't be bought for a price or found by the wicked. It can be found only by those who truly seek God and travel on the "Highway of Holiness." We receive this "double portion of prosperity and joy" not only during our travels, but also for eternity. Our eternal inheritance cannot be taken away. It is built on the solid-rock foundation of our Lord and Savior, Jesus Christ. These are the only things that will last—not the things of this world.

Jeremiah also gives us a good piece of advice about our earthly joy: "When I discovered your words, I devoured them. They are my joy and my heart's delight, for I bear your name, O LORD God of Heaven's Armies."[9] This verse is a key element in living a life filled with the things of the Spirit and not the flesh. God's Word is our owner's manual for life and a road map that leads us on the "Highway of Holiness."

Believers, if you want to live a life that is pleasing to the Lord, you have to know the Word to discover what pleases him. His Word is our lifeline and our food. It is our source of information on how we are to live a life empowered by the Spirit and not enslaved to the flesh. We have to know his Word. There is no other way. When you study his Word, you feed your spirit and starve your flesh. Let's go one step further. His Word has to be in your mind, but more importantly, in your heart.

Here is another big key to experiencing joy in your life. Jesus said, "When you obey me, you remain in my love, just as I obey my Father and remain in his love. I have told you this so that you will be filled with my joy. Yes, your joy will overflow!"[10] Do you get what this verse is saying? If you obey his Word, you will not only be filled with joy but with *his* joy. This truly unspeakable, incomprehensible joy will overflow.

Here is the way to have this type of joy: *obedience*. If you live in obedience to his Word, you understand the type of joy and spiritual inheritance that are hard even to describe. If you are not currently living in obedience to his Word, I highly recommend doing it. You may think it might mean sacrificing your wants and desires (flesh), but I can assure you from my personal experience, it is not a sacrifice at all.

Some other ways that the Bible describes the joy that comes from God and not from the world include complete, something no one can rob you of, glorious, and inexpressible. The kind of joy that is described in the verses above is definitely not of this world.

The joy that we have spoken of in these verses is a fruit of the Holy Spirit.

But when the Holy Spirit controls our lives, he will produce this kind of fruit in us; love, joy, peace, patience, kindness, goodness, faithfulness, gentleness, and self-control.[11]

Fruit is developed when we feed our spirits and starve our flesh. The only way we can experience the joy the Bible describes is by living empowered by the Holy Spirit. When we feed and nourish our spirits, our spirits will be empowered to have inexpressible joy. When we don't feed our spirits, the flesh will be empowered to have sorrow. When we don't live in the Spirit, our automatic human default setting is the opposite of the Holy Spirit's attributes. Again, the one that wins is the one that is fed. Which one are you feeding? Your appetite, cravings, and diet have earthly and eternal consequences.

NOTES

1   Nehemiah 8:10 NLT
2   Psalm 16:11 NLT
3   Psalm 51:12 NLT
4   Psalm 97:11 NLT
5   Proverbs 10:28 NIV
6   Isaiah 51:11 NLT
7   Isaiah 35:8 NLT
8   Isaiah 61:7 TLB
9   Jeremiah 15:16 NLT
10 John 15:10 and 11 NLT
11 Galatians 5:22 TLB

CHAPTER 6

Peace Vs Strife

The next result of our choice to live in the Spirit or in the flesh is peace or strife. Are you going to live each day empowered by the Spirit to have peace or enslaved by the flesh to have strife?

First, I want to discuss the meaning of peace. The world describes peace as the opposite of war or absence of conflicts. Again, the world has its type of peace based only on external circumstances and not internal attributes. The world cannot obtain peace, but as a child of God we have internal peace that is freely given to us when we make peace with God through accepting his Son, Jesus Christ.

Even if flesh-driven people have peace, it is temporary and based on their circumstances rather than on their core being. No wonder there is so much anger, war, strife, and out-of-control behavior in the world today. The peace that the world tries to obtain is beyond its reach.

Let's discuss the definition that the Bible gives for peace. The Hebrew word for *peace* used in several of the verses we are going to discuss is *shalom*, which means completeness or to be whole. Wow! So basically the bottom line here is unless we have the peace that is given only through Jesus Christ, we are not whole. I can relate to the feeling of incompleteness, a void, or emptiness I had before I met Jesus Christ.

I tried to fill that void with so many facets of the world, but I couldn't. Now, I have a wholeness or completeness that can be explained only by the relationship I have with Jesus Christ. It is not dependent on circumstances or surroundings, but on the inheritance I received when the Holy Spirit came to dwell within my flesh. I received a peace, which is a fruit of the Spirit, when I was forgiven of my sins. That peace continues to be magnified when I feed my spirit and starve my flesh. The fruit of the Spirit, which I have developed and matured through my relationship with Jesus Christ, continues to produce more peace than I can even describe.

Now that we have discussed how the world's peace and our peace as Spirit-filled Christians are vastly different, let's look at what the Bible says about the peace that we receive as part of our spiritual inheritance. In Psalms, we read, "The Lord gives his people strength. The Lord blesses them with his peace."[1] Did you get that? He gives his people strength and blesses them with his peace. Isn't it truly a blessing to have the choice to obtain his peace?

The Bible also says that the peace given by God will not be taken away. "Though the mountains be shaken and the hills be removed, yet my unfailing love for you will not be shaken nor my covenant of peace be removed, says the Lord, who has compassion on you."[2]

Psalms also says, "Those who love your instructions have great peace and do not stumble."[3] This verse talks about not only peace, but great peace. This great peace comes from loving the law. Loving the law is a result of your obedience to the law. Ultimately, obedience leads to a life that is so blessed internally that it is hard to keep it to yourself. People will notice a difference in you and want what you have. I guarantee it.

The Bible also says, "Deceit fills hearts that are plotting evil; joy fills hearts that are planning peace!"[4] The Bible tells us that we are blessed with a great peace and that through promoting peace, we have joy, as we saw in the previous chapter. Wow! The benefits continue to be amazing for us as Spirit-filled Christians.

Let's also look at this verse, "They don't know where to find peace or what it means to be just and good. They have mapped out crooked roads, and no one who follows them knows a moment's peace."[5] Based on this verse, sinners cannot know a moment's peace. Can you imagine not having a moment of peace? If we, as Christians, didn't have this internal peace, we would be just like the world: tired, stressed, irritable, and unable to handle each day without an outburst. Does that sound familiar in the world we live? The lost need help, and we have the only answer that can truly help cure their problems. It is the Great Physician, Jesus Christ, who is just a call or "knee-mail" away. Show them the cure before it is too late.

In John, Jesus said, "I am leaving you with a gift—peace of mind and heart. And the peace I give is a gift the world cannot give. So don't be troubled or afraid."[6] Jesus refers to peace of mind and heart as a gift. I strongly agree that this peace of mind and heart is a gift and can be experienced only by his children.

Peace of mind and heart are also found in this verse: "Don't worry about anything; instead, pray about everything. Tell God what you need, and thank him for all he has done. Then you will experience God's peace, which exceeds anything we can understand. His peace will guard your hearts and minds as you live in Christ Jesus."[7]

If you follow the words from these verses and do not worry, but pray, how would that change your life? I can speak to this first-hand. I am living proof of how this truth can change a life. If we realize that worrying is the symptom of a much greater problem, we can try to diagnose and treat the underlying problem. Worrying is the ultimate result of not trusting God to handle the issue at hand. If we trusted God completely, we would pray and give it to him and let him handle it. By telling God what we need and thanking him for all he has done, we will experience God's peace which the world can't understand nor buy! It is priceless!

And let the peace that comes from Christ rule in your hearts. For as members of one body you are called to live in peace. And always be thankful.[8]

With God's peace ruling our hearts, our hearts and minds are guarded. We can live a life of freedom from worry and all that results from it, like anxiety, stress, anger, bitterness, depression, strife, frustration, and many others—a cascade of trouble in your life. Now don't get me wrong here. We will have trouble in this life, but God is with us to help us through these troubled times.

"I have told you these things, so that in me you may have peace. In this world you will have trouble. But take heart! I have overcome the world."[9]

Not only do we have peace, we are on the winning team. God has overcome the world. If you know this, why would you not choose to be a child of God? The world doesn't understand that being a child of God is not a sacrifice at all. If you truly experience God's forgiveness, grace and mercy in your life, you will never be the same. The middle letter for sin and pride is *i*. The world says it is all about me. But with every kick the world has to offer, there is a kickback—a consequence that must be paid either here on earth, in eternity, or both.

Do you realize that living obediently to the law is worth the amazing internal inheritance and protection we get while here on earth? These things can't be bought for a price but are given freely to all who ask with sincere hearts. God doesn't play favorites and is not partial to some; everyone has equal access.

Favoritism Breeds Division, But Equality Breeds Unity.

Since God doesn't play favorites, nor should we. "Work at living in peace with everyone, and work at living a holy life, for those who are not holy will not see the Lord."[10] We need to live at peace and live a holy life so we will see God. If we don't see God, we will have made the biggest mistake of our lives, which results in eternal separation from God in hell.

The Bible says, "So letting your sinful nature control your mind leads to death. But letting the Spirit control your mind leads to life and peace."[11] Here the apostle Paul divides people into two categories: those who are controlled by their sinful natures (flesh) and those who are controlled by the Holy Spirit (Spirit). If we hadn't taken Jesus up on his offer to free us from our sins, we would still be controlled by our flesh. Constantly, we have to crucify the sinful nature and feed our spirits to empower the Spirit to control our lives. Then and only then can we have *true* life and peace.

But when the Holy Spirit controls our lives he will produce this kind of fruit in us: love, joy, peace, patience, kindness, goodness, faithfulness, gentleness and self-control.[12]

These traits are displayed in us when we have healthy, well-fed, and energized spirits. These traits are also a description of Christ. We are called to be more Christ-like while here on earth and to make an invisible God more visible to a lost world.

Are you displaying the fruit of a healthy spirit, or are you displaying the negative attributes of the flesh? You can only choose one. Which one are you living most like? Are you going to live empowered by the Spirit to have peace, or enslaved to the flesh to have strife in your life? The choice is yours. I pray that after seeing the results of your choice, you will choose peace. The way you are living now will have an earthly and eternal impact on you and most likely, on those around you!

NOTES

1   Psalm 29:11 NLT
2   Isaiah 54:10 NIV
3   Psalm 119:165 NLT
4   Proverbs 12:20 NLT
5   Isaiah 59:8 NLT
6   John 14:27 NLT
7   Philippians 4:6 and 7 NLT
8   Colossians 3:15 NLT
9   John 16:33 NIV
10 Hebrews 12:14 NLT
11 Romans 8:6 NLT
12 Galatians 5:22 TLB

CHAPTER 7

Patience Vs Impatience

The next result of our choice to live in the Spirit or in the flesh is patience or impatience. Are you going to live each day empowered by the Spirit to have patience or enslaved by the flesh to have impatience?

Let's first look at the definition of patience. To be patience is to be even-tempered and long-suffering. This attribute can only be tested under trial. The apostle Paul said this in his letter to the Corinthian church:

In fact, in everything we do we try to show that we are true ministers of God. We patiently endure suffering and hardship and trouble of every kind. We have been beaten, put in jail, faced angry mobs, worked to exhaustion, stayed awake through sleepless nights of watching, and gone without food. We have proved ourselves to be what we claim by our wholesome lives and by our understanding of the Gospel and by our patience. We have been kind and truly loving and filled with the Holy Spirit.[1]

You can see that the trials these early Christians had to go through helped them prove themselves as they exhibited attributes that could be empowered only by the Spirit and not the flesh. When you are patient, you are showing a very important Christ-like attribute.

Since God chose you to be the holy people whom he loves, you must clothe yourselves with tenderhearted mercy, kindness, humility, gentleness, and patience.[2]

This next verse in the Old Testament talks about the suffering and trials of the prophets and of the Lord's servant: "For examples of patience in suffering, dear brothers and sisters, look at the prophets who spoke in the name of the Lord. We give great honor to those who endure under suffering.

For instance, you know about Job, a man of great endurance. You can see how the Lord was kind to him at the end, for the Lord is full of tenderness and mercy."[3] Before the Holy Spirit was ever sent to people after Jesus's ascension to heaven, the prophets and Job displayed patience. Today, we have a helper—the Holy Spirit—within each one of us, which Jesus said he would send after he ascended into heaven. We, as post-resurrection Christians, have the help of the Holy Spirit in us to display patience.

The last part of the verse mentioned above deserves another look. It says that from Job's experience, we can see how God's plan ended in good. Similarly, we read in Romans: "And we know that God causes everything to work together for the good of those who love God and are called according to his purpose for them."[4]

This is one of the most freeing concepts in the Word of God. God's good *always* comes out of life's bad. Did you get that? I didn't say *sometimes* but *always*. Now this truth is only reserved for those who love God and are living the purpose he created them to fulfill. I am not saying that God's good can't come out of life's good, but when good comes from bad, God gets more glory. You see, like Job, we can't always understand God's plans, but rest assured, he understands and knows best.

Let me give you a couple of examples about this concept of God's good coming from life's bad. First, the disciples and other believers who saw Jesus after his resurrection couldn't have possibly understood why he had to leave them and go to heaven. After all, what could be better than seeing him rise from the dead to be alive on earth.

If he had stayed here on earth, he would have been limited to his humanness, his flesh, and to being in only one place at a time. By going to heaven, he could send his Holy Spirit, who could be omnipresent (all places at all times) because he would no longer be confined to his flesh. Through his Spirit, he could be with and within each of us intimately at all times and in all places. That is a better plan and a good example of how God's good *always* comes out of life's bad.

We find another example in the apostle Paul. After his amazing conversion on the road to Damascus, Paul was called to bring the Good News to the Gentiles and to plant churches. But Paul spent a lot of time in prison and couldn't do what he was called to do. During his imprisonment, he wrote numerous letters to churches that he had started or planned to start after his release from prison, which then became books in the New Testament. These letters have had an amazing impact on Christians today, over two thousand years later. If he had not been in prison, he might not have written all the beautiful letters that are in the New Testament and that instruct our lives as Christians today. This is another example of how God's good *always* comes out of life's bad.

Now let's get back to patience. Patience is also defined as "an ability or willingness to suppress restlessness or annoyance when confronted with delay: to have patience with a slow learner."[5] As far as giving my life to Christ was concerned, I took a long time to learn the hard way that I needed him in my life and to be in control of my life. Even after forty years of waiting, he was right there when I asked him to come into my life. Now that is patience.

The apostle Paul also referred to God's patience in this verse:

Christ Jesus came into the world to save sinners—and I was the worst of them all. But that is why God had mercy on me, so that Christ Jesus could use me as a prime example of his great patience with even the worst sinners. Then others will realize that they, too, can believe in him and receive eternal life.[6]

God is patient with us because he is still giving sinners time to repent. He doesn't want anyone to have to live without his eternal presence, otherwise known as hell. The Bible says:

"Don't you realize how patient he is being with you? Or don't you care? Can't you see that he has been waiting all this time without punishing you, to give you time to turn from your sin? His kindness is meant to lead you to repentance."[7]

Peter also spoke of this patience: "And remember, our Lord's patience gives people time to be saved."[8] The Bible also says, "In the same way, even though God has the right to show his anger and his power, he is very patient with those on whom his anger falls, who are destined for destruction."[9] God can return at any moment, and then it will be too late for repentance.

The Lord isn't really being slow about his promise, as some people think. No, he is being patient for your sake. He does not want anyone to be destroyed, but wants everyone to repent.[10]

So he waits patiently for sinners to turn from their sins to him.

We also need to show patience while waiting for God's timing and not ours. He will test us to see how our character and endurance handle the waiting period. In these times, we need to have faith that he knows best and that his timing is perfect.

David spoke about waiting on God several times in Psalms:

Be still in the presence of the Lord, and wait patiently for him to act. Don't worry about evil people who prosper or fret about their wicked schemes.[11]

He also speaks of waiting in this verse: "I waited patiently for the Lord to help me, and he turned to me and heard my cry."[12] David tells us to be still and to wait for God to act. With all the distractions we have in our lives today, to be still in this world is very abnormal. Because of all the busyness with life and distractions from technology, it is very difficult to find a place and a time where we can be still before God. I truly believe that if you can be still and silent before God, you will know not only that he is God, but you will know God.

Be still, and know that I am God![13]

The wait strengthens not only our patience but also our faith. Patience is truly a fruit of the Holy Spirit.

But when the Holy Spirit controls our lives, he will produce this kind of fruit in us; love, joy, peace, patience, kindness, goodness, faithfulness, gentleness, and self-control.[14]

Such fruits are developed when we feed our spirits and starve our flesh. The only way to experience the patience described in this chapter is to live empowered by the Holy Spirit and not enslaved to the flesh. So I challenge all Christians with this verse: "This means that God's holy people must endure persecution patiently, obeying his commands and maintaining their faith in Jesus."[15]

NOTES

1   2 Corinthians 6:4–6 NLT
2   Colossians 3:12 NLT
3   James 5:10 and 11 NLT
4   Romans 8:28 NLT
5   "Patience / Define Patience at Dictionary.com" accessed June 8, 2018. https://www.dictionary.com/browse/patience.
6   1 Timothy 1:15 and 16 NLT
7   Romans 2:4 TLB
8   2 Peter 3:15 NLT
9   Romans 9:22 NLT
10   2 Peter 3:9 NLT
11   Psalm 37:7 NLT
12   Psalm 40:1 NLT
13   Psalm 46:10 NLT
14   Galatians 5:22 NLT
15   Revelations 14:12 NLT

CHAPTER 8

Kindness Vs Cruelty

The next result of our choice to live in the Spirit or in the flesh is kindness or cruelty. Are you going to live each day empowered by the Spirit to be kind or enslaved by the flesh to be cruel?

Let's first take a look at the definition of kindness. Kindness means having a good or benevolent nature, being considerate, helpful, mild, gentle, compassionate, and gracious, and having a sympathetic attitude towards others.[1] Most people would say that they desire to have these qualities and to relate to people with this type of nature.

The opposite of kind is cruel. I don't know if you have noticed, but the world today is far from kind. People are all about me, myself, and I. Nothing else in life really matters but getting personal needs met as instantaneously as possible.

People are busier, more stressed out, and more distracted today than ever before. It just seems to be getting worse. What happened to relationships in the family? What happened to eating dinner together? What happened to the old, classic television shows and movies? What happened to children being able to run around and play outside without constant parental supervision due to the fear of someone abducting them? What happened to telephone conversations, handwritten notes, and lunch dates? Our world has become so distracted with technology and productivity that we are missing the real meaning of life, which is relationships.

Relationships are the only thing of lasting value that we can invest in, here on the earth, but we don't relate anymore. Our children are not going to know how to have a normal conversation with another person because they communicate via texting, social media, instant messaging, and other impersonal ways. If they can't even have a telephone conversation with another person, how are they going to know how to relate to people face-to-face? The upcoming generation is going to be in a world of hurt because they don't know how to have a real relationship—one in which they listen, talk, see nonverbal behaviors, and hear the tone of another person's voice. These important aspects of communication are not part of our children's normal everyday conversations and relationships.

Without relationships, we really can't show kindness to anyone. Kindness is an action, and if we don't relate to others, we can't show them kindness. I truly believe Satan has devised this plan to get and keep us so distracted from relationships that we will become comfortable with the impersonal way we relate to people. He is doing everything in his evil power to keep us so busy and distracted that we don't relate to each other.

When we don't relate to people, we can't show them Jesus. If we can't show them Jesus and all his characteristics, we can't show them what they are missing without a relationship with him. If we can't show them what they are missing, we miss the opportunity to provide them with the most important information to make the most important decision in their lives. If they don't give their lives to Christ, we aren't able to help expand God's kingdom. We have missed out on the one real purpose we were left on earth to accomplish after becoming children of God.

With all that being said, I hope you see how we need to show others Christ through our actions and relationships. An important characteristic of Christ is his kindness.

He gives his king great victories; he shows unfailing kindness to his anointed, to David and his descendants forever.[2]

The Bible also speaks of the Lord's kindness:

In a surge of anger I hid my face from you for a moment, but with everlasting kindness I will have compassion on you, says the Lord Redeemer.[3]

But let the one who boasts boast about this: that they have the understanding to know me, that I am the LORD, who exercises kindness, justice and righteousness on earth, for in these I delight, declares the LORD.[4]

The Lord specifies here that he shows and exercises unfailing and everlasting kindness and delights in it. The Lord also speaks of leading us with kindness.

I led Israel along with my ropes of kindness and love. I lifted the yoke from his neck, and I myself stooped to feed him.[5]

He leads us with ropes of kindness and love. Sometimes his leading requires a tight rope; sometimes he allows us some slack. When we are going off in our own direction and not staying on the path he has intended for us to travel, he pulls the rope tight so he can lead us back. This can be a painful tug to get our attention, but it is always with our best interests in mind.

Sometimes, the rope can have a little slack because we are following his perfect will and path. He can trust us to stay close and trust him. We know from past experiences or from wisdom that he will never lead us astray. Sometimes we need to be fed along the way. He feeds us what we need because he is a God of provision. He does this all with everlasting and unfailing kindness.

I also like what this verse says about kindness: "So God can point to us in all future ages as examples of the incredible wealth of his grace and kindness toward us, as shown in all he has done for us who are united with Christ Jesus."[6] God shows favor to his children. Along with his favor, he shows us his incredible kindness.

I don't know about you, but I see God's hand of favor in my life every day. Usually, it's in the little things like waiting in line at the grocery store or at a restaurant. I always see how he gets me in line before an incredible crowd forms behind me. Sometimes, I get a close parking space at the busiest spot in town or get a break in traffic at just the right time.

When this happens, I always try to remember and thank him for his incredible hand of favor in my life. In addition to thanking him, I tell my daughter of God's favor so that she sees his hand at work in my life, in hopes that she will recognize him in her life. This not only strengthens her faith but also impacts her, her family, and the spiritual legacy I want to leave behind.

The Bible also speaks of God's kindness in Romans. "Notice how God is both kind and severe. He is severe to those who disobeyed, but kind to you as you continue to trust in his kindness. But if you stop trusting, you also will be cut off."[7] God can be kind and severe: kind when we continue to trust in his kindness, severe when we are disobedient or stop trusting in him and his kindness. Then your rope will be cut. I don't know about you, but I don't want my rope or lifeline to be cut.

Now let's look at another verse about kindness:

Let the godly strike me! It will be a kindness! If they correct me, it is soothing medicine. Don't let me refuse it. But I pray constantly against the wicked and their deeds.[8]

Here David said that being rebuked by a godly person is kindness. I agree with him. God speaks through others and might be trying to help us see an area in our life that we need to change. **Nobody Likes Criticism, but When it is Given Wisely and Taken Humbly, it Will be a Benefit.**

David suggested that the way to deal with criticism was to consider it as a kindness. Don't fight back and don't refuse it. Then you will benefit from it in a constructive versus a destructive manner, regardless of the original intent.

In the same way God is kind, we are called to be kind.

We prove ourselves by our purity, our understanding, our patience, our kindness, by the Holy Spirit within us, and by our sincere love.[9]

Here, the apostle Paul said that the way we prove ourselves to be Christians is to have certain attributes, one being kindness.

Since God chose you to be the holy people whom he loves, you must clothe yourselves with tenderhearted mercy, kindness, humility, gentleness, and patience.[10]

We are his representatives and have an important responsibility to accurately portray his true and holy character.

The kindness spoken of in these verses is a fruit of the Holy Spirit.

But when the Holy Spirit controls our lives, he will produce this kind of fruit in us; love, joy, peace, patience, kindness, goodness, faithfulness, gentleness, and self-control.[11]

Again, fruit is developed when we feed our spirits and starve our flesh. The only way to experience the kindness that I have discussed in this chapter is by living empowered by the Holy Spirit and not being enslaved to the flesh. The choice is yours. I pray that after seeing the results of your choice, you will choose kindness. Your choice will have an earthly and an eternal impact.

NOTES

1   "Kind / Define Kind at Dictionary.com" accessed July 1, 2018. https://www.dictionary.com/browse/kind.
2   2 Samuel 22:51 NIV
3   Isaiah 54:8 NIV
4   Jeremiah 9:24 NIV
5   Hosea 11:4 NLT
6   Ephesians 2:7 NLT
7   Romans 11:22 NLT
8   Psalm 141:5 NLT
9   2 Corinthians 6:6 NLT
10 Colossians 3:12 NLT
11 Galatians 5:22 NLT

CHAPTER 9

Righteousness Vs Wickedness

The next result of our choice to live in the spirit or in the flesh is righteousness and wickedness. Are you going to live each day empowered by the Spirit to be righteous or enslaved by the flesh to be wicked?

Let's first take a look at the definition of righteousness. It means to be morally right, justifiable, honest, blameless, innocent, guiltlessness, purity, of the utmost integrity, and virtuous.[1] Unfortunately, in the world today, we don't find many people who display the characteristics of righteousness. Wickedness or evil is the norm, and it is the dominating force in the world.

Satan is the ringleader of evil and wickedness in the world. The Bible says that he is the "prince of this world." In John we read: "Now is the time for judgment on this world; now the prince of this world will be driven out."[2] Satan is an angel who rebelled against God, a real spiritual force who is constantly working against God and those who obey God. Satan tempted Eve to sin in the garden of Eden.

We are all sons and daughters of Adam and Eve, so we are born as sinners. We can be delivered from the power of sin and from Satan by the victory that Jesus Christ won on the cross. Satan is powerful, but Jesus is omnipotent—unlimited or infinite power.

But you belong to God, my dear children. You have already won a victory over those people, because the Spirit who lives in you is greater than the spirit who lives in the world.[3]

Righteousness comes only by faith in Jesus Christ and not by keeping the rules of the law.

And Abram believed the Lord, and the Lord declared him righteous because of his faith.[4]

Although Abram had demonstrated his faith through his actions, his belief in the Lord and not his actions made him right with God.

We can also have a right relationship with God by trusting in him. Our outward actions can be good and right, like going to church, serving in ministry, and reading and studying his Word, but those actions by themselves do not make us right with God. In fact, the Bible says our acts of righteousness are filthy rags when compared with God's righteousness.

We are all infected and impure with sin. When we display our righteous deeds, they are nothing but filthy rags.[5]

A right relationship with God is based on our heart's condition. We must have an innermost trust and confidence that God is who he says he is and does what he says he will do. As we have faith in God and our relationship with him grows and matures, our right actions will be a product of that faith in God.

We are made right with God by placing our faith in Jesus Christ. And this is true for everyone who believes, no matter who we are. For everyone has sinned; we all fall short of God's glorious standard.[6]

We are only able to be right if we accept the free gift of forgiveness of our sins through Jesus Christ. Jesus is the only one who can forgive us and make us righteous.

For God presented Jesus as the sacrifice for sin. People are made right with God when they believe that Jesus sacrificed his life, shedding his blood. This sacrifice shows that God was being fair when he held back and did not punish those who sinned in times past, for he was looking ahead and including them in what he would do in this present time. God did this to demonstrate his righteousness, for he himself is fair and just, and he declares sinners to be right in his sight when they believe in Jesus.[7]

So you see, only by believing in Jesus can we be made right in God's sight.

God is righteous, loves righteousness, rewards righteousness, and will judge in righteousness. Let's first discuss his righteousness. In Psalms we read: "Righteousness and justice are the foundation of your throne. Unfailing love and truth walk before you as attendants."[8] His foundation is righteousness.

Your righteousness is like the mighty mountains, your justice like the ocean depths.[9]

The Bible also says, "Your righteousness, O God, reaches to the highest heavens. You have done such wonderful things. Who can compare with you, O God?"[10] And we are also assured of this: "Everything he does reveals his glory and majesty. His righteousness never fails,"[11] and "His righteousness is everlasting."[12]

In these verses God's righteousness is compared to the mighty mountains and the highest heavens, and is the foundation of his throne, unfailing and everlasting. Now who can compare with that? No one, praise your name, oh God!

Now let's look at how he loves righteousness.

The Lord loves righteousness and justice; the earth is full of his unfailing love.[13]

God loves righteousness and hates wickedness.

You love righteousness and hate wickedness; therefore God, your God, has set you above your companions by anointing you with the oil of joy.[14]

We see from that verse that we who are righteous will be set above our companions by being anointed with the oil of joy.

The Bible speaks of his love for righteousness in this verse as well: "The Lord detests the way of the wicked, but he loves those who pursue righteousness."[15] God is righteous and loves all who are righteous. Now don't get me wrong on this point. God loves each of us, but the majority of the world does not live in righteousness, but wickedness.

Remember, God cannot be in the presence of sin, so when we are in sin, we cannot be close to God, and therefore, we must accept the only way to him. This only way is through the forgiveness of our sins and the acceptance of his Son, Jesus Christ, who died to pay the price for each of our sins.

He personally carried away our sins in his own body on the cross so we can be dead to sin and live for what is right. You have been healed by his wounds![16]

Then and only then, can we be close to God. Through our relationship with him, we become more like him. When we become more like him, we begin to display his qualities. One of those qualities is righteousness. If we are not close to God, we live in our natural, sinful flesh, which is wicked through and through.

Now let's take a look at how our righteousness is rewarded.

The wicked man earns deceptive wages, but the one who sows righteousness reaps a sure reward. The truly righteous man attains life, but he who pursues evil goes to his death.[17]

We are rewarded not only with eternal life but also with abundant life while we are here on earth.

Whoever pursues righteousness and unfailing love will find life, righteousness, and honor.[18]

We find life, righteousness, and honor. But see what else we get with our pursuit of righteousness.

Those who are wise will shine as bright as the sky, and those who turn many to righteousness will shine like stars forever.[19]

Many would do anything to be a star in today's world. All the fame and fortune that the entertainment industry provides make it look as if this stardom would provide the ultimate fulfillment and satisfaction in life. But have you noticed that these worldly stars are the most miserable people in the world? They turn to drugs, alcohol, and other addictions when they find that ultimate fame and fortune do not fill the void that they still have.

God gives us a way to be a star for eternity and not just temporarily. This type of star will have the ultimate fulfillment and satisfaction on earth and for eternity. This type of eternal stardom is rewarded to those who point many people to righteousness.

The ultimate reward is spoken of in this verse: "Seek the Kingdom of God above all else, and live righteously, and he will give you everything you need."[20] We have to put God above everything else in our lives: relationships, money, sex, and all other things that the world deems as important. If we put God first in our lives, his kingdom and his righteousness will be ours as well. Now that is quite an inheritance. Not only that, but you will be filled with a satisfaction and fulfillment that all the things of the world cannot provide. Ultimately, we have made a choice to live for eternal rewards instead of earthly things, which also leads to earthly fulfillment and satisfaction.

Lastly, let's take a look at how each of us will be judged when Christ returns.

For the Lord is coming! He is coming to judge the earth. He will judge the world with righteousness and all the nations with his truth.[21]

The Lord will judge each of us with righteousness. The only way we can escape this judgment is to be forgiven of our sins through the blood of his Son, Jesus Christ.

So now there is no condemnation for those who belong to Christ Jesus.[22]

We have been freed of our guilt and the sentence of death row. As humans, we are all on death row, and our only escape from death is to accept the free gift of freedom, which was bought with the shedding of Jesus Christ's blood on the cross for our sins. If we accept him who took the punishment, we can be made right and will not be eternally punished for our sins. Then we will be righteous in his sight.

And Christ lives within you, so even though your body will die because of sin, the Spirit gives you life because you have been made right with God.[23]

The righteousness that we have spoken of in these verses is a fruit of the Holy Spirit.

But when the Holy Spirit controls our lives, he will produce this kind of fruit in us; love, joy, peace, patience, kindness, goodness, faithfulness, gentleness, and self-control.[24]

So goodness, which is also known as righteousness, is also a fruit of the Spirit. Fruit is developed when we feed our spirits and starve our flesh. The only way to experience the righteousness that we have referred to in this chapter is by living empowered by the Holy Spirit and not being enslaved to the flesh. The choice is yours. I pray that after seeing the results of your choice, you will choose righteousness. Your choice will have an earthly and an eternal impact.

Lastly, I want to touch on the breastplate of righteousness, which is part of our spiritual armor that we are to wear every day to protect us from the evil spiritual forces that surround and attack us.

For we are not fighting against flesh-and-blood enemies, but against evil rulers and authorities of the unseen world, against mighty powers in this dark world, and against evil spirits in the heavenly places. Therefore, put on every piece of God's armor so you will be able to resist the enemy in the time of evil. Then after the battle you will still be standing firm. Stand your ground, putting on the belt of truth and the body armor of God's righteousness. For shoes, put on the peace that comes from the Good News so that you will be fully prepared. In addition to all of these, hold up the shield of faith to stop the fiery arrows of the devil. Put on salvation as your helmet, and take the sword of the Spirit, which is the word of God.[25]

The spiritual armor mentioned in these verses is key to our victory in the constant battle of spirit versus flesh. The body armor of righteousness is our defense against evil forces. Are you fighting this battle with your spiritual armor on? If so, you will find that your days of victory are more than your days of defeat in this constant spiritual battle.

NOTES

1   "Righteousness / Define Righteousness at Dictionary.com" accessed July 5, 2018. https://www.dictionary.com/browse/righteousness

2   John 12:31 NIV

3   1 John 4:4 NLT

4   Genesis 15:6 NLT

5   Isaiah 64:6 NLT

6   Romans 3:22 and 23 NLT

7   Romans 3:25 and 26 NLT

8   Psalm 89:14 NLT

9   Psalm 36:6 NLT

10 Psalm 71:19 NLT

11 Psalm 111:3 NLT

12 Psalms 119:42 NIV

13 Psalm 33:5 NIV

14 Psalm 45:7 NIV

15 Proverbs 15:9 NIV

16 1 Peter 2:24 NLT

17 Proverbs 11:18 and 19 NIV

18 Proverbs 21:21 NLT

19 Daniel 12:3 NLT

20 Matthew 6:33 NLT

21 Psalm 96:13 NLT

22 Romans 8:1 NLT

23 Romans 8:10 NLT

24 Galatians 5:22 NLT

25 Ephesians 6:12–17 NLT

CHAPTER 10

Gentleness Vs Harshness

The next result of our choice to live in the Spirit or in the flesh is gentleness and harshness. Are you going to live each day empowered by the Spirit to be gentle or enslaved by the flesh to be harsh?

First, let's take a look at the definition of gentleness. Gentleness is defined as kind, meek, polite, fair, moderate, tamed, quiet, courteous, polished, and refined.[1] I don't know about you, but I would like people to characterize me this way. I would also like to treat others this way. But in the world today, this is not how the majority of people behave. It is not in our natural, sinful, selfish nature to act in gentleness, but to act in harshness or cruelness. We have to be empowered by the Holy Spirit to be gentle.

Gentleman is not a term that is used in today's culture like it was in the past. We have all forgotten about the qualities we want in others and in ourselves as well. Where are all the gentlemen and gentlewomen in the world today? Everyone is concerned about me, myself, and I. That is why the world is in such discord. No one cares about anything or anyone above themselves. The uncaring and harshness we find in today's culture are frightening, to say the least.

Jesus Christ displayed the ultimate gentleness and meekness while he was here on earth over two thousand years ago. We all need to follow his example as his representatives today. If we did, we would stand out and show the world a different way to live today. I think this trait could be one that would win someone over to Jesus Christ as much as, if not more than, a lot of the other traits Jesus Christ portrayed.

People in the world today are looking for the gentleness and meekness in their relationships and are having a hard time finding it. If we step forward as representatives of Jesus Christ and show and treat someone with gentleness, we will make a friend. Through that friendship, we can earn the trust to share why we are different and how that person can get what we have—Jesus Christ. I challenge each of us to go out into the world with a gentleness that will be noticed by everyone.

Now let's take a look at some scriptures that talk about gentleness. In Proverbs we read: "A gentle answer turns away wrath, but a harsh word stirs up anger."[2] Wow! I love that verse. Did you get that? It says that if we answer in a gentle way, we turn away wrath. But if we answer with harsh words, we stir up anger. Have you ever tried to argue in a whisper? It doesn't work.

Harsh words stir up anger, and anger causes voices to rise and emotions to take over. Then we say and do things that we often regret later. Some of these things we do and say in an emotional state of anger cause lifetime scars and regrets for the giver and receiver of the words and/or actions. Do you see how being gentle while dealing with others can keep us from starting or participating in an argument? Often after an argument, we don't even remember what we were arguing about, but we do remember the harsh words said or actions done.

Jesus Christ said, "Take my yoke upon you. Let me teach you, because I am humble and gentle at heart, and you will find rest for your souls."[3] Jesus Christ described himself as gentle. If he used that term to describe himself and he was perfect, then we should strive to be gentle as well. Jesus's gentleness is also described in this next verse: "See, your king comes to you, gentle and riding on a donkey, and on a colt, the foal of a donkey."[4]

The Bible describes the Creator of the universe and the Savior of the world as a king, but then as gentle and riding on a colt. Does that fit the picture that you have in your mind of a king who is the Creator and Savior of the world? No, this is contrary to what the world thinks that an all-knowing, all-powerful, all-present Creator and Savior of the universe should be. I would think that he would descend from the clouds, riding on a white horse where all could see him and would be announced with trumpet blasts where all could hear the coming of the King of glory, Jesus Christ. This is the way he will come the second time, but it was not the first.

He chose a lowly animal and manner of entering the world the first time. He seemed to be defeated the first time he was on the earth, but we know that he rose from the dead, is living in heaven, and is sitting at the right hand of God the Father. While he is there, he is preparing a place for us. He will return in victory to judge all for the way that they have chosen to live their lives.

How will the judgment be for you? Will you bow your knee in humble adoration and confess with your mouth that Jesus Christ is Lord with thankfulness, or will you bow your knee in humble adoration and confess with your mouth that Jesus Christ is Lord out of fear and regret because of the choices you made while on earth? Notice, all of us will bow and confess, the only thing that will be different will be the way we feel doing it—thankful or fearful! The Bible says, "that at the name of Jesus every knee shall bow in heaven and on earth and under the earth, and every tongue shall confess that Jesus Christ is Lord, to the glory of God the Father."[5] Please make your choice to follow him now before it is too late.

The apostle Paul asked the church of Corinth this question: "Which do you choose? Should I come with a rod to punish you, or should I come with love and a gentle spirit?"[6] We don't know if Paul actually returned to the church at Corinth or not, but he asked them these questions because they were having conflicts among themselves, taking sides, and forming small groups led by different preachers. Each group thought its beliefs were the only truth, and each had become spiritually arrogant and proud.

There is a time and a place for punishment and scolding and a time and place for quiet love and gentleness. But the best way to handle most situations is to punish with gentleness and always display quiet love. That way, the wrath of others won't come out as much and emotions and tempers won't start flaring. The result of this type of punishment would more than likely be a constructive rather than a destructive outcome. The underlying intent of the punishment would be achieved without scars and regrets.

In this next verse, the apostle Paul tells us how to act as one who has been called by God: "Always be humble and gentle. Be patient with each other, making allowance for each other's faults because of your love."[7] We are living as good representatives of Christ when we live as humble and gentle people, are patient with each other, and accept each other's faults because of the love we have for Jesus Christ.

It is so easy in the flesh to point out other's faults but not to see our own. None of us are perfect. We all have faults. We won't be perfect until we are promoted to heaven. Until that time, we are being refined to become more like Christ. In our refining, there will be fire that will bring out our impurities.

We Are Refined From the Inside Out, Not the Outside In.

This next verse also refers to the called and chosen people of God: "Since God chose you to be the holy people whom he loves, you must clothe yourselves with the tenderhearted mercy, kindness, humility, gentleness, and patience. You must make allowance for each other's faults and forgive the person that offends you. Remember, the Lord forgave you, so you must forgive others."[8]

Again, we are to clothe ourselves with the qualities that set us apart from the world and make us good representatives of Jesus Christ. These are the qualities that make a person beautiful and not the things that the world calls beautiful like outer appearance, money, possessions, fame, and status. These things are only temporary and will fade away.

Peter wrote this verse: "You should be known for the beauty that comes from within, the unfading beauty of a gentle and quiet spirit, which is so precious to God."[9] Unfading, true beauty comes from within through refinement by becoming more like Christ and less like our selves. Then it is revealed to the world from the inside out. The qualities that please God will last eternally and grow more beautiful with aging, unlike the temporary outer qualities of the world. The world's outer self might appear beautiful, but the inside can be dark and unsightly.

God's Word says you are a wonderfully, complex work who was formed with his watchful eye. He knew you and what your life would be before you were born. His thoughts toward you are precious and are more than the number of grains of sand. He is always with you. Now who can compare to that? No one. No one else's words or opinions really matter if you are living according to God's standard and not the world's. The standards of the world conflict with the standards of God.

You made all the delicate inner parts of my body and knit me together in my mother's womb. Thank you for making me so wonderfully complex! Your workmanship is marvelous—and how well I know it. You watched me as I was being formed in utter seclusion, as I was woven together in the dark of the womb. You saw me before I was born. Every day of my life was recorded in your book. Every moment was laid out before a single day had passed. How precious are your thoughts about me, O God! They are innumerable! I can't even count them; they outnumber the grains of sand! And when I wake up in the morning, you are still with me![10]

The apostle Paul also described gentleness in this way: "Nor did we seek glory from people, whether from you or from others, though we could have made demands as apostles of Christ. But we were gentle among you, like a nursing mother taking care of her own children."[11] I like that description of how gentleness looks. A mother feeding and caring for her own children is a perfect description of how gentleness should appear. God views us as his own children and deals with us in a gentle manner out of his unconditional, unfailing love.

The apostle Paul also refers to gentleness when he is writing to Timothy about the qualities of a church leader: "He must not be a heavy drinker or be violent. He must be gentle, not quarrelsome, and not love money."[12] If we are to lead others, we need to display these qualities in order to be a good example of Jesus Christ and a good leader. Actions speak louder than words. We are held responsible for the people God puts in our sphere of influence. If we lead them astray from God and his Word, we will be held accountable.

The gentleness that we have spoken of in these verses is a fruit of the Holy Spirit.

But when the Holy Spirit controls our lives, he will produce this kind of fruit in us; love, joy, peace, patience, kindness, goodness, faithfulness, gentleness, and self-control.[13]

Fruit is developed when we feed our spirits and starve our flesh. The only way to experience the gentleness that we have referred to in this chapter is by living empowered by the Holy Spirit and not enslaved to the flesh. The choice is yours. I pray that after seeing the results of your choice, you will choose gentleness. Your choice will have an earthly and an eternal impact.

NOTES

1   "Gentleness / Define Gentleness at Dictionary.com" accessed July 8, 2018. <u>https://www.dictionary.com/browse/righteousness</u>

2   Proverbs 15:1 NIV

3   Matthew 11:29 NLT

4   Matthew 21:5 NIV

5   Philippians 2:10 and 11 TLB

6   1 Corinthians 4:21 NLT

7   Ephesians 4:2 NLT

8   Colossians 3:12 and 13 NLT

9   1 Peter 3:4 NLT

10 Psalm 139:13–18 NLT

11 1 Thessalonians 2:6 and 7 *English Standard Version* (ESV)

12 1 Timothy 3:3 NLT

13 Galatians 5:22 NLT

CHAPTER 11

Faithfulness Vs Unfaithfulness

The next result of our choice to live in the Spirit or in the flesh is faithfulness versus unfaithfulness. Are you going to live each day empowered by the Spirit to be faithful or enslaved by the flesh to be unfaithful?

Let's first look at the definition of faithfulness. Faithfulness is defined as true, devoted, constant, loyal, dependable, trusted, steadfast, and reliable.[1] These are qualities that any relationship of value should contain. When we love God, we want to be faithful to him because he has been faithful to us. His Word is true. Since the beginning of time, He has proven that his faithfulness can be trusted. The Bible defines faith this way in Hebrews: "Faith shows the reality of what we hope for; it is the evidence of things we cannot see."[2]

We are the problem. Our flesh is not naturally faithful but the opposite. We have to rely on the Holy Spirit, who lives in each of us because we are God's children, to provide us with the ability to be faithful in our relationship with God and each other.

God's faithfulness toward us has been proven over time. His very nature only allows him to be true to his Word. His faithfulness is described in these verses:

The Lord passed in front of Moses, calling out, "Yahweh! The Lord! The God of compassion and mercy! I am slow to anger and filled with unfailing love and faithfulness."[3]

Your unfailing love, O Lord, is as vast as the heavens; your faithfulness reaches beyond the clouds.[4] For the LORD is good. His unfailing love continues forever, and his faithfulness continues to each generation.[5]

God's faithfulness and unfailing love are not in question, but ours is. The "wall of faith" in the Bible can be found in Hebrews 11. It shows that there must be action behind our faith.

This is what the ancients were commended for.

By faith we understand that the universe was formed at God's command, so that what is seen was not made out of what was visible.

By faith Abel brought God a better offering than Cain did. By faith he was commended as righteous, when God spoke well of his offerings. And by faith Abel still speaks, even though he is dead.

By faith Enoch was taken from this life, so that he did not experience death: "He could not be found, because God had taken him away." For before he was taken, he was commended as one who pleased God. And without faith it is impossible to please God, because anyone who comes to him must believe that he exists and that he rewards those who earnestly seek him.

By faith Noah, when warned about things not yet seen, in holy fear built an ark to save his family. By his faith he condemned the world and became heir of the righteousness that is in keeping with faith.

By faith Abraham, when called to go to a place he would later receive as his inheritance, obeyed and went, even though he did not know where he was going. By faith he made his home in the promised land like a stranger in a foreign country; he lived in tents, as did Isaac and Jacob, who were heirs with him of the same promise. For he was looking forward to the city with foundations, whose architect and builder is God. And by faith even Sarah, who was past childbearing age, was enabled to bear children because she considered him faithful who had made the promise. And so from this one man, and he as good as dead, came descendants as numerous as the stars in the sky and as countless as the sand on the seashore.

All these people were still living by faith when they died. They did not receive the things promised; they only saw them and welcomed them from a distance, admitting that they were foreigners and strangers on earth. People who say such things show that they are looking for a country of their own. If they had been thinking of the country they had left, they would have had opportunity to return. Instead, they were longing for a better country—a heavenly one. Therefore God is not ashamed to be called their God, for he has prepared a city for them.

By faith Abraham, when God tested him, offered Isaac as a sacrifice. He who had embraced the promises was about to sacrifice his one and only son, even though God had said to him, "It is through Isaac that your offspring will be reckoned." Abraham reasoned that God could even raise the dead, and so in a manner of speaking he did receive Isaac back from death.

By faith Isaac blessed Jacob and Esau in regard to their future.

By faith Jacob, when he was dying, blessed each of Joseph's sons, and worshiped as he leaned on the top of his staff.

By faith Joseph, when his end was near, spoke about the exodus of the Israelites from Egypt and gave instructions concerning the burial of his bones.

By faith Moses' parents hid him for three months after he was born, because they saw he was no ordinary child, and they were not afraid of the king's edict.

By faith Moses, when he had grown up, refused to be known as the son of Pharaoh's daughter. He chose to be mistreated along with the people of God rather than to enjoy the fleeting pleasures of sin. He regarded disgrace for the sake of Christ as of greater value than the treasures of Egypt, because he was looking ahead to his reward. By faith he left Egypt, not fearing the king's anger; he persevered because he saw him who is invisible. By faith he kept the Passover and the application of blood, so that the destroyer of the firstborn would not touch the firstborn of Israel.

By faith the people passed through the Red Sea as on dry land; but when the Egyptians tried to do so, they were drowned.

By faith the walls of Jericho fell, after the army had marched around them for seven days.

By faith the prostitute Rahab, because she welcomed the spies, was not killed with those who were disobedient.

And what more shall I say? I do not have time to tell about Gideon, Barak, Samson and Jephthah, about David and Samuel and the prophets, about David and Samuel and the prophets, who through faith conquered kingdoms, administered justice, and gained what was promised; who shut the mouths of lions, quenched the fury of the flames, and escaped the edge of the sword; whose weakness was turned to strength; and who became powerful in battle and routed foreign armies. Women received back their dead, raised to life again. There were others who were tortured, refusing to be released so that they might gain an even better resurrection. Some faced jeers and flogging, and even chains and imprisonment. They were put to death by stoning; they were sawed in two; they were killed by the sword. They went about in sheepskins and goatskins, destitute, persecuted and mistreated—the world was not worthy of them. They wandered in deserts and mountains, living in caves and in holes in the ground.

These were all commended for their faith, yet none of them received what had been promised, since God had planned something better for us so that only together with us would they be made perfect.[6]

There Are More Benefits to Being in the Hall of Faith than the Hall of Fame.

Wow! Need I say more? If any of us had faith like one of these listed above on the "wall of faith," we would be able to move mountains. What is holding us back? Oh yeah, me, myself, and I.

The faith in these verses is a fruit of the Holy Spirit.

But when the Holy Spirit controls our lives, he will produce this kind of fruit in us; love, joy, peace, patience, kindness, goodness, faithfulness, gentleness, and self-control.[7]

Fruit is developed when we feed our spirits and starve our flesh. The only way to experience the faithfulness found in this chapter is by living empowered by the Holy Spirit and not enslaved to the flesh. The choice is yours. I pray that after seeing the results of your choice, you will choose faithfulness. Your choice will have an earthly and an eternal impact.

NOTES

1 "Faithfulness / Define Faithfulness at Dictionary.com" accessed July 12, 2018. https://www.dictionary.com/browse/faithfulness.
2 Hebrews 11:1 NLT
3 Exodus 34:6 NLT
4 Psalm 36:5 NLT
5 Psalms 100:5 NLT
6 Hebrews 11:2–40 NLT
7 Galatians 5:22 NLT

CHAPTER 12

Self-Control Vs Uncontrolled

The next result of our choice to live in the Spirit or in the flesh is self-control versus uncontrolled. Are you going to live each day empowered by the Spirit to be self-controlled or enslaved by the flesh to be uncontrolled?

Let's first take a look at the definition of self-control. Self-control means the control of one's own desires, actions, or emotions by one's own will. Other words that mean the same thing are self-discipline, self-restraint, willpower, and levelheadedness.[1]

I want to stress the importance of understanding what self-control is. If we want to be able to control ourselves in a way that is pleasing to God, we have to be controlled by the Spirit and not by the self. We can do some things in our own will, but the things that are pleasing to God come through spiritual control and not self-control. In order to be self-controlled, we first have to be spirit controlled. The self will lead us to an uncontrolled state of mind where we live out the desires of the flesh and not the Spirit.

In Proverbs, it says, "A person without self-control is as defenseless as a city with broken-down walls."[2] Back in Old Testament days, a city's walls were viewed as its protection and security. Without them, the city would be vulnerable to attacks by its enemies. We can view our self-control as walls of defense and protection that keep us within healthy boundaries. An uncontrolled or out-of-control life is subject to all forms of vulnerabilities and attacks, which lead to destruction. We need walls and healthy boundaries to provide protection in our lives from ourselves and others.

The apostle Paul talked about the dangers of the last days in his letter to Timothy. I want you to see how this is a description of the world we live in today. Paul wrote this about two thousand years ago:

You should know this, Timothy, that in the last days there will be very difficult times. For people will love only themselves and their money. They will be boastful and proud, scoffing at God, disobedient to their parents, and ungrateful. They will consider nothing sacred. They will be unloving and unforgiving; they will slander others and have no self-control; they will be cruel and have no interest in what is good. They will betray their friends, be reckless, be puffed up with pride, and love pleasure rather than God. They will act as if they are religious, but they will reject the power that could make them godly. You must stay away from people like that.[3]

Wow! This is such an accurate description of how the world and its people live today. Remember, we are called to be in the world but not of the world. If we are truly living in a way that is Spirit-controlled, we will definitely stand out in this world of evil and darkness and our light will not go unnoticed. The world today serves the worldly trinity of me, myself, and I versus the Holy Trinity of the Father, the Son, and the Holy Spirit. We will discuss this more in detail in a later chapter.

Peter talked about self-control in his second book in the Bible. It is used in reference to our growth in the knowledge of God.

His divine power has given us everything we need for a godly life through our knowledge of him who called us by his own glory and goodness. Through these he has given us his very great and precious promises, so that through them you may participate in the divine nature, having escaped the corruption in the world caused by evil desires. For this very reason, make every effort to add to your faith goodness; and to goodness, knowledge; and to knowledge, self-control; and to self-control, perseverance; and to perseverance, godliness; and to godliness, mutual affection; and to mutual affection, love. For if you possess these qualities in increasing measure, they will keep you from being ineffective and unproductive in your knowledge of our Lord Jesus Christ. But whoever does not have them is nearsighted and blind, forgetting that they have been cleansed from their past sins.[4]

Do you see what Peter is saying to us in these verses? Self-control is part of the spiritual maturity process. These verses are a road map to spiritual maturity. How is your spiritual journey going? Are you progressing, backsliding or just staying stagnate in your walk with God? We need to all do a self-check and have accountability from other Christians in our life to help us assess our walk and make sure we are progressing in the right direction.

Paul also wrote a letter to Titus instructing him on how to teach various groups.

You, however, must teach what is appropriate to sound doctrine. Teach the older men to be temperate, worthy of respect, self-controlled, and sound in faith, in love and in endurance. Likewise, teach the older women to be reverent in the way they live, not to be slanderers or addicted to much wine, but to teach what is good. Then they can urge the younger women to love their husbands and children, to be self-controlled and pure, to be busy at home, to be kind, and to be subject to their husbands, so that no one will malign the word of God. Similarly, encourage the young men to be self-controlled.[5]

Here Paul emphasized the importance of right teaching. We, as believers, must be grounded in the truth of God's Word so that we won't be moved by false teaching, the possible devastation of tragic circumstances, or the pull of our emotions.

We have to be grounded in the truth and do what God's Word calls us to do. The older people should teach the younger people by their words, but more importantly, by their examples and actions. This is how values and truth are passed down from generation to generation. You can see in Paul's words to Titus that self-control is an important attribute to have and to teach to others.

We need the wisdom and discernment that come by mastering our minds, wills, emotions, and our passions so that Christ will be honored. Peter calls us to holy living in this verse: "So prepare your minds for action and exercise self-control. Put all your hope in the gracious salvation that will come to you when Jesus Christ is revealed to the world."[6]

We are to be mentally alert and self-controlled while we await the return of Jesus Christ. The imminent return of Christ should motivate us to continually surrender everything to and for him.

Peter also spoke of the end times in this verse as well: "The end of all things is at hand; therefore, be self-controlled and sober-minded for the sake of your prayers."[7] All things will be destroyed in the end. The only things that are eternal are the relationships we have invested in here on earth and the eternal rewards we will receive in heaven for the work we have done for

Christ. The things of this world (the seen) will be no more. The unseen will be eternal. Don't focus your energies on things that are seen and temporary, but focus on things that are unseen and eternal.

The self-control described in these several verses is a fruit of the Holy Spirit.

But when the Holy Spirit controls our lives, he will produce this kind of fruit in us; love, joy, peace, patience, kindness, goodness, faithfulness, gentleness, and self-control.[8]

Fruit is developed when we feed our spirits and starve our flesh. The only way to experience the self-control referred to in this chapter is by living empowered by the Holy Spirit and not enslaved by the flesh. The choice is yours. I pray that after seeing the results of your choice, you will choose self-control. Your choice will have an earthly and an eternal impact.

NOTES

1   "Self Control / Define Self Control at Dictionary.com" accessed July 15, 2018.
     https://www.dictionary.com/browse/self-control.
2   Proverbs 25:28 NLT
3   2 Timothy 3:1–5 NLT
4   2 Peter 1:3–9 NIV
5   Titus 2:1–6 NIV
6   1 Peter 1:13 NLT
7   1 Peter 4:7 ESV
8   Galatians 5:22 NLT

CHAPTER 13

Humility Vs Pride

The next result of our choice to live in the Spirit or in the flesh is humility versus pride. Are you going to live each day empowered by the Spirit to be humble or enslaved by the flesh to be prideful?

Let's first look at the definition of humility. It is defined as "not proud or arrogant, modest, having a feeling of insignificance, inferiority, and low in rank or importance and status."[1] The opposite of humility is pride. In the world today, most people are full of pride. Humility is a rarity in our culture. The middle letter in pride and sin is *i*. It is all about me, myself, and I.

When we realize that it is not about you or me but all about him, we become humble. Through humility God can work in amazing ways in our lives.

Moses wrote in Deuteronomy:

Remember how the LORD your God led you all the way in the wilderness these forty years, to humble and test you in order to know what was in your heart, whether or not you would keep his commands. He humbled you, causing you to hunger and then feeding you with manna, which neither you nor your ancestors had known, to teach you that man does not live on bread alone but on every word that comes from the mouth of the LORD.[2]

The Lord used the forty years in the wilderness to humble and test the Israelites. It took Moses days to lead the Israelites out of Egypt, but it took God years to get Egypt out of the Israelites. Even after spending forty years in the wilderness, the Israelites continued to live in disobedience to God and his Word. Even after seeing the miraculous parting of the Red Sea, the cloud during the day, and the pillar of fire at night, which signified his presence, they still did not humble themselves before the almighty God. Even with the daily provision of bread from heaven, they still complained and focused on themselves and not on him.

Most people think that life is about satisfying their appetites. Whether your appetite is for money, materialism, fame, sex, drugs, alcohol, or anything else your appetite desires, you will find that these things will not satisfy you at all. In fact, they will leave you more empty and dissatisfied. We still have a fleshly tendency to focus on *me* and not *he*. When we do this, we lose sight of what real life is all about. It is about him and not about you or me and our needs.

The Israelites did not pass the test that God put them through in the wilderness. How are you doing with the test God has given you? Are you passing or failing? Just as in school, if you fail the test, you will have to take it again. Remember, God tests, but Satan tempts.

In Samuel we read: "You rescue those who are humble, but your eyes watch the proud and humiliate them."[3] God rescues the humble but humiliates the proud. He also leads and teaches the humble.

He leads the humble in doing right, teaching them his way.[4]

He also supports the humble.

The Lord supports the humble, but he brings the wicked down into the dust.[5]

He also crowns the humble with salvation.

For the LORD delights in his people; he crowns the humble with victory.[6]

The Lord also shows favor to the humble.

The Lord mocks proud mockers but shows favor to the humble and oppressed.[7]

The Lord will also bless the humble.

My hands have made both heaven and earth; they and everything in them are mine. I, the LORD, have spoken! "I will bless those who have humble and contrite hearts, who tremble at my word."[8]

The Lord will protect the humble.

Seek the LORD, all who are humble, and follow his commands. Seek to do what is right and to live humbly. Perhaps even yet the LORD will protect you—protect you from his anger on that day of destruction.[9]

The Lord will have the humble on his holy mountain.

And then you will no longer need to be ashamed of yourselves, for you will no longer be rebels against me. I will remove all your proud and arrogant people from among you; there will be no pride or haughtiness on my holy mountain. Those who are left will be the poor and the humble, and they will trust in the name of the Lord.[10]

The Lord lifts up the humble.

He has brought down princes from their thrones and exalted the humble.[11]

The humble receive wisdom.

Pride leads to disgrace, but with humility comes wisdom.[12]

Do you see the benefits that come when we have humility before our God? He will rescue, lead, teach, support, crown, favor, bless, protect, exalt, and provide wisdom. The humble will be left alive when the end comes. Hallelujah, praise our God!

Jesus was humble in his flesh as well as his spirit, and we are called to be like him. Jesus said, "Take my yoke upon you. Let me teach you, because I am humble and gentle at heart, and you will find rest for your souls."[13] Jesus chose to leave heaven and be born in a manger into a family with a modest lifestyle at best. He chose his mother, Mary, who was a fifteen-year-old virgin, and Joseph, who was a carpenter by trade.

Though he was God, he did not think of equality with God as something to cling to. Instead, he gave up his divine privileges; he took the humble position of a slave and was born as a human being. When he appeared in human form.[14]

He could have chosen anyone to be his earthly parents, but he chose two people who were not worth much in the world's view. Mary said in Luke, "For he took notice of his lowly servant girl, and from now on all generations will call me blessed."[15] Lowly can also be interpreted as humble. Of all the women on earth in that day, Jesus chose a lowly servant girl to be his earthly mother.

Then he chose to live the modest life of a carpenter's family until he started his ministry at thirty years of age. When Jesus was about to be crucified, he rode a donkey's colt into Jerusalem.

Tell the people of Israel, "Look, your King is coming to you. He is humble, riding on a donkey-even on a donkey's colt."[16]

Then Jesus died a criminal's death on a cross for your sins and mine.

He humbled himself in obedience to God and died a criminal's death on a cross.[17]

His earthly life was not a life of wealth, luxury, and pleasure. It was a humble life that fulfilled one purpose. That purpose was to pay the price for our sins so that we could be back in relationship with God and not have to face eternal punishment. How amazing it is that this perfect man would suffer such excruciating pain and humility out of love for us. Jesus lived his earthly life as a perfect example of humility and purpose, completely empowered by the Spirit, and crucified to the flesh. If Jesus lived this way, how much more should we?

But, dear children, that is not the way he will come next time. In Revelation we read: "Look! He comes with the clouds of heaven. And everyone will see him—even those who pierced him. And all the nations of the world will mourn for him. Yes! Amen!"[18] Next time Jesus comes, it will not be as a humble, earthly teacher. He will come as our glorious, all-powerful, victorious King and God. Jesus's second coming will be victoriously visible, and everyone will know who he is.

In Philippians, the apostle Paul wrote, "Therefore, God elevated him to the place of highest honor and gave him the name above all other names, that at the name of Jesus every knee should bow, in heaven and on earth and under the earth, and every tongue confess that Jesus Christ is Lord, to the glory of God the Father."[19] Did you get that? *Every* knee will bow, and *every* tongue will confess that Jesus Christ is Lord.

You can choose to commit your life to Jesus and to live a humble life full of meaning and purpose now, or you can be forced to acknowledge him at his return. Let me warn you, however, that the choice you make will have eternal consequences. I pray, my friend, that you will choose to commit your life to him now and before it is too late. He is coming back soon. Are you ready?

NOTES

1   "Humble / Define Humble at Dictionary.com" accessed July 30, 2018. https://www.dictionary.com/browse/humble.

2   Deuteronomy 8:2 and 3 NIV

3   2 Samuel 22:28 NLT

4   Psalm 25:9 NLT

5   Psalm 147:6 NLT

6   Psalm 149:4 NLT

7   Proverbs 3:34 NIV

8   Isaiah 66:2 NLT

9   Zephaniah 2:3 NLT

10 Zephaniah 3:11 and 12 TLB

11 Luke 1:52 NLT

12 Proverbs 11:2 NLT

13 Matthew 11:29 NLT

14 Philippians 2:6 and 7 NLT

15 Luke 1:48 NLT

16 Matthew 21:5 NLT

17 Philippians 2:8 NLT

18 Revelation 1:7 NLT

19 Philippians 2:9–11 NLT

CHAPTER 14

Purity Vs Impurity

The next result of our choice to live in the Spirit or in the flesh is purity versus impurity. Are you going to be empowered each day by the Spirit to live in purity or be enslaved by the flesh to live in impurity?

Let's first look at the best definition I have ever found for the word *purity* in a book by Josh McDowell, which says to be pure sexually is to "live according to God's original design."[1] Wow! That is powerful. But I think we could take this definition and apply it to every facet of our lives. Do you remember back in the beginning when we talked about God's original design? His design was for us to be in complete fellowship with him and in his presence, but due to our sin, we became separated from him. So living in purity is living according to God's original design.

The Bible says, "Because we have these promises, dear friends, let us cleanse ourselves from everything that can defile our body or spirit. And let us work toward complete purity because we fear God."[2] This verse explains the cleansing process as being twofold. The first step is turning from your sin, and the second step is turning toward God.

This verse tells us to work toward complete purity because we fear God. Purity is not only about your body, but also about your thoughts and actions. Purity is about a state of mind, an attitude, and a way to live. It affects every aspect of our lives: physical, emotional, mental, spiritual, and relational. We do this because we have the fear, which means reverence or respect, of God and want to do what is pleasing to him.

The Bible also says, "The Lord despises the thoughts of the wicked, but he delights in pure words."[3] And it also talks about thoughts in this verse:

"Fix your thoughts on what is true and honorable and right. Think about things that are pure and lovely and admirable. Think about things that are excellent and worthy of praise."[4]

You see, what we put in our minds determines what comes out in what we say and do. Examine what you are putting in your mind from television, computers, magazines, books, movies, and relationships with others. I want you to understand how important it is to guard your minds. Here is the result of what goes into your mind: Thoughts lead to actions, which lead to behaviors, which lead to attitudes, which lead to habits. It all starts in the mind.

Don't copy the behavior and customs of this world, but let God transform you into a new person by changing the way you think. Then you will know what God wants you to do, and you will know how good and pleasing and perfect his will really is.[5]

I make it a daily practice in my time with God every morning to ask him to keep a watch over my mind and to be the gatekeeper of all my thoughts. I submit authority of all my thoughts to Jesus Christ and ask him to allow exclusive entrance to thoughts that are pleasing to him. This practice helps keep me focused on the eternal and not earthly things.

Aim at and seek the rich, eternal treasures that are above ... And set your minds and keep them set on what is above ... not on the things that are on the earth ... kill the evil desires and all that is earthly in you.[6]

The Bible also tells us how a young person can stay pure: "By obeying your word."[7] Do you remember how we talked about rules without a relationship leading to rebellion? Our relationship grows by spending time with Jesus Christ through Bible study, prayer, journaling, meditating on God's Word, serving, and fellowshipping with other Christians. When you spend time with someone, you get to know him or her and even become more like that person. When we spend time with Jesus, we feed the Holy Spirit and empower him to lead us instead of our flesh leading us. Then and only then, can we obey the rules. We can't do it in our own strength.

We are living in a world that is drowning in impurity. Everywhere we turn, we see things that tempt us from living in a way that pleases the Lord. God says:

But remember that the temptations that come into your life are no different from what others experience. And God is faithful. He will keep the temptation from becoming so strong that you can't stand up against it. When you are tempted, he will show you a way out so that you will not have to give in to it.[8]

So when you are tempted, look for the way out. Temptation is not a sin, but giving into it is. Jesus was tempted but never gave into it.

Temptations come from Satan. As a child of God, Satan and his demonic forces have to get permission from God before they can tempt us. The temptations that are allowed by God are tests. God is able to see our true character when we are tempted. Patience can't be tested until there is a heated situation that causes us to want to be impatient. Our impurities come out best in the refining heat of a fire. If we don't pass a test from God, we will most likely have to retake it. Ouch!

The Bible also instructs: "Run from anything that stimulates youthful lust. Follow anything that makes you want to do right. Pursue faith and love and peace, and enjoy the companionship of those who call on the Lord with pure hearts."[9] So remove yourself from weak spots that stimulate you to sin. Knowing when to run is just as important as knowing how and when to fight.

Now that we have talked about what purity is and ways to stay pure in this impure world, let's talk about why we should want to be pure. The Bible says, "Who may climb the mountain of the LORD? Who may stand in his holy place? Only those whose hands and hearts are pure, who do not worship idols and never tell lies."[10] It also says, "Blessed are the pure in heart, for they will see God."[11] I don't know of any other place in the Bible where it states the result of a pure heart so clearly. We will *see God!*

Not only will we see God, but we can be near him while here on earth.

Draw close to God, and God will draw close to you. Wash your hands, you sinners; purify your hearts, you hypocrites.[12]

God comes near to us when we draw near to him. If there is distance between you and God, you need to check yourself because God is always faithful to be near his children. We are the ones that move away from God.

This verse shows how actions speak much louder than words: "We have proved ourselves by our purity, our understanding, our patience, our kindness, our sincere love, and the power of the Holy Spirit."[13] The power of the Holy Spirit gives us the ability to live in a pure way.

This verse talks about how a godly woman who is married to an ungodly man can change him: "Your godly lives will speak to them better than any words. They will be won over by watching your pure, godly lives."[14] Because we have been left here to lead others to Christ, the best way of doing this is to live in a pure way. By leading pure lives, we are making an invisible God more visible!

Now I ask you, what will it be for you? Will you be empowered by the Spirit to live in a pure way or be enslaved by the flesh to live in impurity? Your choice will have an earthly and eternal impact.

NOTES

1 Josh McDowell, *The Bible Handbook of Difficult Verses: A Complete Guide to Answering the Tough Questions* (Eugene: Harvest House Publishers, 2013), 288.
2 2 Corinthians 7:1 NLT
3 Proverbs 15:26 NLT
4 Philippians 4:8 NLT
5 Romans 12:2 NLT
6 Colossians 3:1, 2 and 5 NLT
7 Psalm 119:9 NLT
8 1 Corinthians 10:13 NLT
9 2 Timothy 2:22 NLT
10 Psalm 24:3 and 4 NLT
11 Matthew 5:8 NLT
12 James 4:8 NLT
13 2 Corinthians 6:6 NLT
14 1 Peter 3:1 and 2 NLT

CHAPTER 15

Satisfied Vs Dissatisfied

The next result of our choice to live in the Spirit or in the flesh is being satisfied versus dissatisfied. Are you going to live each day empowered by the Spirit to be satisfied or to be enslaved by the flesh to be dissatisfied?

The world today looks for immediate satisfaction or gratification. This type of satisfaction is temporary at best and usually results in some type of kickback—pain, hangovers, regrets, guilt, and so on. Our flesh cannot be satisfied.

God created us with a longing in the deepest core of our beings that only he can reach and fill. He did this so we would continually search until we found him. This void in our heart can't be filled by anything or anyone else but him. Trust me, I know.

As I mentioned in my story, I tried it *all* and came up emptier every time. My life song during that season of my life, which may be many of yours, were the words, "I can't get no satisfaction," from the song "Satisfaction" by The Rolling Stones. God was what I had been relentlessly searching for all along. He was right there with opened arms when I asked him to help me. That is a true example of unfailing love and patience.

Let's look at the definition of satisfaction. It means "contentment, pleasure, gratification, fulfillment, enjoyment, and happiness."[1] This is what most people deep down in the core of their innermost beings desire. However, most people don't know what God provides to *all* who ask and receive it, which deeply burdens me.

The satisfaction that the Lord provides is not a temporary thing. It is eternal. Unlike our flesh, we need to continually eat and drink to keep from being hungry and thirsty. We need to keep having sex in order to fulfill our fleshly desires. We need more money because what we have is never enough. We need to keep drinking alcohol, smoking marijuana, or doing other drugs because the high doesn't last.

The Bible talks about a satisfaction that is lasting and that doesn't need to be replaced. In Matthew we read: "God blesses those who hunger and thirst for justice, for they will be satisfied."[2] Jesus was speaking to the Samaritan woman at the well in this verse: "If you only knew the gift God has for you and who you are speaking to, you would ask me, and I would give you living water."[3]

God is called "the fountain of life"[4] and "the fountain of living water."[5] Here Jesus said he will satisfy the soul with the water that he provides. This *living water* quenches our *thirst* so we no longer desire the things of the world. I know that I have drunk from this cup. Have you? If not, what are you waiting for? Drink, before it is too late.

I want to share a story with you. This is one of the few times I have felt the Holy Spirit speak to my soul so closely. I was in Venezuela on a mission trip several years ago. The sponsors always provided us with bottled water (*agua* in Spanish) because we could have gotten sick if we had drunk the tap water.

One day, we were holding a Vacation Bible School for the children in someone's front yard. It was hot that day, and I took a drink from my bottle of water. This precious little Venezuelan girl tugged on me (and my heart) and said, "*Agua.*"

So I leaned down, took the cap off the bottle, poured a little water in the cap, and held it to her mouth so she could drink it. The Holy Spirit spoke to my heart and said, "When you give to the least of these, it is like giving to me." Water not only came from the bottle but streamed from my eyes as well. This was one of the most powerful moments of my life.

So yet again, I ask you, what will you choose? Will you be empowered by the Spirit to live in satisfaction or enslaved by the flesh to live in dissatisfaction? I pray you choose to live satisfied and drink from the cup of living water that only Jesus provides. Your choice will have an earthly and eternal impact.

NOTES

1   "Satisfaction / Define Satisfaction at Dictionary.com" accessed August 10, 2018. https:// www.dictionary.com/browse/satisfaction.

2   Matthew 5:6 NLT

3   John 4:10 NLT

4   Psalm 36:9 NLT

5   Jeremiah 2:13 NLT

CHAPTER 16

Rest Vs Stress

The next result of our choice to live in the Spirit or in the flesh is rest versus stress. Will you live each day empowered by the Spirit to live in rest or enslaved by the flesh to live in stress?

The definition of rest is "sleep, freedom from labor or activity, being motionless, and death."[1] The flesh will never have enough rest. We constantly need sleep and rest to survive another day. Again, our flesh is never satisfied.

In God's Word, rest has several different meanings. Let's take a look at the first one. In Genesis, we read: "On the seventh day God had finished his work of creation, so he rested from all his work."[2] This passage speaks of the seventh day of creation. Another verse says, "For all who have entered into God's rest have rested from their labors, just as God did after creating the world."[3] This passage speaks about the Sabbath, which is a day of rest for the children of God. This type of rest is physical.

The next type of rest in the Word of God is found in Psalms 95:

Come, let us sing to the Lord! Let us shout joyfully to the Rock of our salvation. Let us come to him with thanksgiving. Let us sing psalms of praise to him. For the Lord is a great God, a great King above all gods. He holds in his hands the depths of the earth and the mightiest mountains. The sea belongs to him, for he made it. His hands formed the dry land too.

Come, let us worship and bow down. Let us kneel before the Lord our maker, for he is our God. We are the people he watches over, the flock under his care. If only you would listen to his voice today! The Lord says, "Don't harden your hearts as Israel did at Meribah, as they did at Massah in the

82

wilderness. For there your ancestors tested and tried my patience, even though they saw everything I did. For forty years I was angry with them, and I said, 'They are a people whose hearts turn away from me. They refuse to do what I tell them.' So in my anger I took an oath: 'They will never enter my place of rest' "[4]

This psalm refers to the Israelites who wandered in the desert for forty years and refused to listen to or to obey God. So he did not let them enter the "Promise Land," which was also known as a place of rest, that he had promised to his children both then and now.

So many of us Christians are not living in the promised land while here on earth. We are still wandering in the desert like the Israelites did because we haven't won the battle between spirit and flesh. We are still trying to gratify our ungodly, fleshly desires, which nothing will satisfy except God. If we would just listen and obey God and his Word, we could cross into and live in our promised land, which is flowing with milk and honey. Once you taste what life is like in the promised land, you will not want to go back to the wilderness. This is the only place here on earth where we will get *complete rest*. This type of rest is both physical and spiritual.

Matthew also spoke of rest: "Then Jesus said, 'Come to me, all of you who are weary and carry heavy burdens, and I will give you rest.' "[5] Jesus frees us from all of our heavy burdens of sin. The rest that Jesus refers to is what we have all been looking for. This rest comes from a relationship with God through Jesus Christ. Once we have peace with God through Jesus Christ, we can experience a rest that never fades or runs out.

Sign me up! Oh wait, I signed up fourteen years ago and have experienced this rest every moment since then. Hallelujah!

I have another story to share from God. This was another time like the water bottle experience when I felt the Holy Spirit speak to my heart. I was in the airport picking up my daughter from a weekend with her father. As I was waiting for her, an old lady walked up with her dog and sat beside me—the dog was in between us. I could not help but notice that the dog was jerking its head around and acting like it was having a seizure. I asked her what was going on with her dog, being the dog lover that I am.

She said, "Well, we are here to pick up his master. He is retired, drives busses to other states, and then flies back home. So he is waiting and watching for him."

With great intent, I watched as his master got off the airplane and approached the dog. I thought, *You are getting ready to get covered in wet doggy kisses.* But no, because as soon as he jumped (dare I even say leaped) into his master's arms, he passed out like he was dead.

Again, the Holy Spirit spoke to my heart closely and said, "That is how it is until my children rest in their Father's, also known as the Master's, arms." Wow! Yet again, water poured from my eyes. It was such a touching moment for me.

So again I ask you, what will you choose? Will you live empowered by the Spirit to have rest or enslaved by the flesh to be stressed? I pray that you will choose *complete* rest. Your choice will have an earthly and eternal impact.

NOTES

1   "Rest/Define Rest at Dictionary.com." Accessed August 20, 2018 https://www.dictionary.com/browse.rest.
2   Genesis 2:2 NLT
3   Hebrews 4:10 NLT
4   Psalm 95:1–11 NLT
5   Matthew 11:28 NLT

Chapter 17

Freedom Vs Slavery

The next result of our choice to live in the Spirit or in the flesh is freedom versus slavery. Are you going to spend each day empowered by the Spirit to live in freedom or enslaved by the flesh to live in slavery?

This verse speaks such truth about living with Christ: "And you will know the truth, and the truth will set you free."[1] Jesus shows us the way to eternal life with God and to have freedom to live fulfilling the purpose that he created each of us for. This is not freedom to do whatever our flesh wants, but freedom from slavery to our flesh. When we start living for God and obeying his Word, our fleshly desires lose their appeal, and the things of righteousness become more important in our lives. Then I am free to be the *me* that Christ wants me to be.

The Holy Spirit gives us freedom from having to keep all the Old Testament laws in order to be saved. We fail most every time we try in our own strength to keep all the laws.

For the Lord is the Spirit, and wherever the Spirit of the Lord is, there is freedom.[2]

Jesus lived a perfect life, never sinned, took the punishment of our sins, and satisfied the law once and for all. So there is no condemnation or judgment for those of us who have accepted Jesus Christ as our Lord and Savior.

So now there is no condemnation for those who belong to Christ Jesus. And because you belong to him, the power of the life-giving Spirit has freed you from the power of sin that leads to death.[3]

One of my personal favorite Bible verses is in John: "So if the Son sets you free, you are truly free."[4] I can personally relate to this verse because of my story of defeat when trying to be good in my own strength. I could do anything I set my mind to, *except* when it came to fleshly desires. I was defeated every time.

The night before I gave my life to Christ, I had been smoking, drinking alcohol, watching porn, and having sex with my boyfriend. The next morning, a Sunday in July of 2004, I looked in the mirror and hated who I was and who I had become. I hated even more that I could not behave myself in my own flesh. That morning, I understood and could relate personally to the verse found in John. After I asked Jesus Christ to come into my life and to be the boss of my life and I surrendered control to him, he freed me from my slavery to myself and my sin. This was true freedom indeed.

These next verses also speak of our freedom in Christ: "But the Scriptures declare that we are all prisoners of sin, so we receive God's promise of freedom only by believing in Jesus Christ."[5] The apostle Paul also referenced freedom in this verse from his letter to the churches in southern Galatia and to Christians all over the world today: "God sent him to buy freedom for us who were slaves to the law, so that he could adopt us as his very own children."[6]

This next verse is key to living in a way that is pleasing to the Lord and not attempting to gratify the flesh: "For you have been called to live in freedom, my brothers and sisters. But don't use your freedom to satisfy your sinful nature. Instead, use your freedom to serve one another in love."[7]

This next verse is in a letter to the believers in Ephesus that Paul wrote while he was in prison—physically but not spiritually: "He is so rich in kindness and grace that he purchased our freedom with the blood of his Son and forgave our sins."[8]

Paul wrote about freedom to encourage a young leader in the church by the name of Timothy: "He gave his life to purchase freedom for everyone. This is the message God gave to the world at just the right time."[9]

Peter, a disciple of Jesus, wrote to encourage Christians everywhere, saying, "For you are free, yet you are God's slaves, so don't use your freedom as an excuse to do evil."[10] Peter wrote another letter to Christians to warn them about false teachers: "They promise freedom, but they themselves are slaves of sin and corruption. For you are a slave to whatever controls you."[11]

Wow! Isn't that true? What controls you? If you look at your bank account and calendar, you can get a good idea of what controls you. If you don't find that tithing and church events are your main priority, you need to perform a heart check.

My favorite Christian quote about freedom is from Beth Moore, which I have already mentioned once earlier, but it is worth mentioning again. "Few truly know the unfailing love of God like the captive set free."[12] Again, I will ask you, what will you choose? Will you be empowered by the Spirit to live in freedom or enslaved by the flesh to live in slavery? The choice is yours. I pray that after seeing the results of your choice, you will choose freedom. Your choice will have an earthly and an eternal impact.

NOTES

1   John 8:32 NLT
2   2 Corinthians 3:17 NLT
3   Romans 8:1 and 2 NLT
4   John 8:36 NLT
5   Galatians 3:22 NLT
6   Galatians 4:5 NLT
7   Galatians 5:13 NLT
8   Ephesians 1:7 NLT
9   1 Timothy 2:6 NLT
10 1 Peter 2:16 NLT
11 2 Peter 2:19 NLT
12 Beth Moore, Breaking Free: *Making Liberty in Christ a Reality in Life* (Nashville: B & H Publishing Group, 2000), 202.

CHAPTER 18

Light Vs Darkness

The next result of our choice to live in the Spirit or in the flesh is light versus darkness. Will you be empowered each day by the Spirit to live in light or enslaved by the flesh to live in darkness?

Darkness is known as the absence of light. Darkness can never overtake light. When there is no light, you don't have any sense of direction and can easily hurt yourself. But when you have light, you can see the direction you are going and any warning signs. You avoid pitfalls, stay within the boundaries, and progress forward.

Jesus Christ said, "I am the light of the world. If you follow me, you won't have to walk in darkness, because you will have the light that leads to life."[1] Then Jesus referred to his children as light in this verse: "You are the light of the world—like a city on a hilltop that cannot be hidden. No one lights a lamp and then puts it under a basket. Instead, a lamp is placed on a stand, where it gives light to everyone in the house. In the same way, let your good deeds shine out for all to see, so that everyone will praise your heavenly Father."[2]

We, as children of God, are the light in this vastly expanding, dark world. We *hide* our light when we don't speak out for Christ, but go along with the crowd, let the sin in our life dim our light, and ignore the needs of others. We are called to be different, to stand out, and to have something that others want.

The Bible also talks about light in this passage: "Your eye is like a lamp that provides light for your body. When your eye is healthy, your whole body is filled with light. But when your eye is unhealthy, your whole body is filled with darkness. And if the light you think you have is actually darkness, how deep that darkness is!"[3]

When you have the light of Jesus in you, your eyes are focused on eternal and not earthly things. We shouldn't have anything to hide as children of God so people can see the light in our eyes that comes from Christ alone. When our vision is clouded by self-serving motives, there is no light in our eyes. Our bodies are filled with deep darkness when we have hidden, evil intentions. Now that is scary.

In his letter to the church in Corinth and to Christians everywhere, the apostle Paul wrote: "So don't make judgments about anyone ahead of time—before the Lord returns. For he will bring our darkest secrets to light and will reveal our private motives. Then God will give to each one whatever praise is due."[4] The light that is mentioned in this verse is from God and will shine on all of us and reveal our innermost heart motives upon his return. Paul said here that we should not judge others because God will settle all accounts upon his second coming.

This should make all of us want Jesus's forgiveness in us and working through us so we can warn others to repent and turn to the Forgiver of our sins—Christ and Christ alone—before it is too late. Jesus said, "I am the way, the truth, and the life. No one can come to the Father except through me."[5]

In 1 Corinthians we read: "For God, who said, 'Let there be light in the darkness,' has made this light shine in our hearts so we could know the glory of God that is seen in the face of Jesus Christ."[6] We, as children of God, have the light shining in our hearts. Wow! How powerful to know that you and I have God's light in us and shining through us. People who are in the darkness are uncomfortable when the light comes because it reveals things that they want to keep hidden.

But their evil intentions will be exposed when the light shines on them, for the light makes everything visible.[7]

The following verse is powerful: "We now have this light shining in our hearts, but we ourselves are like fragile clay jars containing this great treasure. This makes it clear that our great power is from God, not from ourselves."[8] This verse shows that we are "fragile clay jars" that house this glorious treasure of light from God, but we can't take credit for it because the light is from God.

Think about a cracked clay pot. Where is the light most visible? The light of God is most visible in the *cracks*, and in those cracks God's glory is powerfully revealed. The cracks are our areas of brokenness where we have had to rely on God's strength to repair them.

Each time he said, "My grace is all you need. My power works best in weakness." So now I am glad to boast about my weaknesses, so that the power of Christ can work through me. That's why I take pleasure in my weaknesses, and in the insults, hardships, persecutions, and troubles that I suffer for Christ. For when I am weak, then I am strong.[9]

Where we are weak, he is strong. The power of Christ is revealed best through our weaknesses.

This next verse talks about the people we are close to in our lives: "Don't team up with those who are unbelievers. How can righteousness be a partner with wickedness? How can light live with darkness?"[10] Other translations use the words, "unequally yoked." This can mean any close relationship like a spouse, boyfriend, girlfriend, or best friend. We have to be careful whom we spend a lot of our time with because we will become like them. This also is true with God. The more time we spend with God, the more we become like him.

In these next verses, we will see that the way we live should resemble those who are in the light: "For once you were full of darkness, but now you have light from the Lord. So live as people of light! For this light within you produces only what is good and right and true."[11] Paul is telling us to live like people of God and not like people of the darkness.

We are known by the way we live and by our actions. The fruit from our lives should be good, right, and true.

But let us who live in the light be clearheaded, protected by the armor of faith and love, and wearing as our helmet the confidence of our salvation.[12]

We need to be clearheaded and not intoxicated by alcohol or drugs in order to feel good or to numb ourselves from the emptiness inside. If we are doing things like this, we are living just like the darkness.

The end of all things is near. Therefore be alert and of sober mind so that you may pray.[13]

Do we want to feel good from the things in this world or because of the one who made this world?

If anyone claims, "I am living in the light," but hates a Christian brother or sister, that person is still living in darkness. Anyone who loves another brother or sister is living in the light and does not cause others to stumble.[14]

We are told to love our other brothers and sisters in Christ and to help them not to fall into sin. Loving others shows the world that we live in the light and not in the darkness.

These next verses speak about our inheritance as children of God who live in the light:

He has enabled you to share in the inheritance that belongs to his people, who live in the light.[15]

But you are not like that, for you are a chosen people. You are royal priests, a holy nation, God's very own possession. As a result, you can show others the goodness of God, for he called you out of the darkness into his wonderful light.[16]

Praise God! We are chosen royalty and children of God. Now that is quite an inheritance that won't fade and can never be taken away. It is our eternal inheritance.

Again I ask you, what will you choose? Will you be empowered by the Spirit to live in the light or enslaved by the flesh to live in the dark? The choice is yours. I pray that after seeing the results of your choice that you will choose light. Your choice will have an earthly and eternal impact.

NOTES

1   John 8:12 NLT
2   Matthew 5:14-16 NLT
3   Matthew 6:22 and 23 NLT
4   1 Corinthians 4:5 NLT
5   John 14:6 NLT
6   2 Corinthians 4:6 NLT
7   Ephesians 5:13 and 14 NLT
8   2 Corinthians 4:7 NLT
9   2 Corinthians 12:9–11 NLT
10   2 Corinthians 6:14 NLT
11   Ephesians 5:8 and 9 NLT
12   1 Thessalonians 5:8 NLT
13   1 Peter 4:7 NIV
14   1 John 2:9 and 10 NLT
15   Colossians 1:12 NLT
16   1 Peter 2:9 NLT

CHAPTER 19

Hope Vs Despair

The next result of our choice to live in the Spirit or in the flesh is to have hope versus despair. Are you going to live each day empowered by the Spirit to have hope or enslaved by the flesh to have despair?

In the book of Matthew we read: "And his name will be the hope of all the world."[1] Jesus is the hope of the world. Our hope lies within us who are here on earth through the power of the Holy Spirit.

I pray that God, the source of hope, will fill you completely with joy and peace because you trust in him. Then you will overflow with confident hope through the power of the Holy Spirit.[2]

Through the power of the Holy Spirit and our personal trust in God, He will fill us completely with joy and peace, and we will overflow with confident hope!

And this hope will not lead to disappointment. For we know how dearly God loves us, because he has given us the Holy Spirit to fill our hearts with his love.[3]

The Holy Spirit has given us the ability to love with God's love. The world doesn't know this kind of love.

One of my favorite verses in the Bible is "But those who hope in the LORD will renew their strength. They will soar on wings like eagles; they will run and not grow weary, they will walk and not be faint."[4] Isn't that a beautiful depiction of what having hope in the Lord produces in each of us? Wow! If you don't have this, don't you want it now?

In Psalms, this verse speaks about our hope in his unfailing love for us: "The LORD delights in those who fear him, who put their hope in his unfailing love."[5] When we fear (revere) the Lord and hope in his unfailing (reliable or constant) love, he delights in us. *Wow!* What an awesome fact: The creator of the universe and the *great I Am* delights in you and me.

Another verse that is quoted quite often and is used in our study of the Word of God is " 'For I know the plans I have for you,' says the Lord. 'They are plans for good and not for disaster, to give you a future and a hope.' " [6] God, who knows all things and is not limited by time, has plans for us. We know that God is trustworthy, so we trust that *his* plans are for our good and for *his* glory. God is with us and for us. This will give us hope now and in the future.

Our hope is also founded on our future eternal life with God in heaven. The following verses speak of this hope:

And we believers also groan, even though we have the Holy Spirit within us as a foretaste of future glory, for we long for our bodies to be released from sin and suffering. We, too, wait with eager hope for the day when God will give us our full rights as his adopted children, including the new bodies he has promised us.[7]

Such things were written in the Scriptures long ago to teach us. And the Scriptures give us hope and encouragement as we wait patiently for God's promises to be fulfilled.[8]

For we have heard of your faith in Christ Jesus and your love for all of God's people, which come from your confident hope of what God has reserved for you in heaven. You have had this expectation ever since you first heard the truth of the Good News.[9]

This verse tells what will always remain: "Three things will last forever—faith, hope, and love—and the greatest of these is love."[10] Faith is defined in this verse: "Now faith is confidence in what we hope for and assurance about what we do not see."[11] We have hope here on earth through the power of the Holy Spirit. We have hope in God's promises that will be fulfilled eternally. The confident hope that we have is earthly and eternal. Our world desperately needs the hope that we have.

Peter spoke about the hope that we have as followers of Christ in this verse: "But in your hearts revere Christ as Lord. Always be prepared to give an answer to everyone who asks you to give the reason for the hope that you have. But do this with gentleness and respect,"[12] We should always be ready to give an answer or to explain the hope that we have because it is contagious—something others want, but don't know how to get. We can explain to them in a gentle and respectful way what Christ has done in and through our lives and why we have hope. It's really hard to hide this type of overflowing hope and joy, which is so needed in the world today.

One of my favorite Christian quotes about hope is from Beth Moore. She said, "Notice the word 'hope' (in Psalm 62:5). The Hebrew term literally means 'a cord, as an attachment.' Every one of us is hanging on to something or someone for security ... if it's someone or something other than God alone, you're hanging on by a thread—the wrong thread."[13]

So I ask you again, what will you choose? Will you live empowered by the Spirit to have hope or enslaved by the flesh to have despair? The choice is yours. I pray that after seeing the results of your choice, you will choose hope. Your choice will have an earthly and eternal impact.

NOTES

1   Matthew 12:21 NLT
2   Romans 15:13 NLT
3   Romans 5:5 NLT
4   Isaiah 40:31 NIV
5   Psalm 147:11 NLT
6   Jeremiah 29:11 NLT
7   Romans 8:23 NLT
8   Romans 15:4 NLT
9   Colossians 1: 4 and 5 NLT
10   1 Corinthians 13:13 NLT
11   Hebrews 11:1 NIV
12   1 Peter 3:15 NIV
13   Beth Moore, *Whispers of Hope: 10 Weeks of Devotional Prayer* (Nashville: B & H Publishing Group, 2013).

CHAPTER 20

Connected Vs Disconnected

The next result of our choice to live in the Spirit or in the flesh is to be connected versus disconnected. Are you going to live each day empowered by the Spirit to be connected or enslaved by the flesh to be disconnected?

We were created by God to live connected to him. The best place for Christians to be is where the Creator and his creations are connected as one. Who knows their creations better than their Creator? When we are connected to God, who has intimately created each of us, we are who he created us to be.

In the Gospel of John we read: "Remain in me, and I will remain in you. For a branch cannot produce fruit if it is severed from the vine, and you cannot be fruitful unless you remain in me. Yes, I am the vine; you are the branches. Those who remain in me, and I in them, will produce much fruit. For apart from me you can do nothing."[1] Did you catch this? If we remain connected to the vine (Jesus Christ), he will remain connected to us. If we are not connected to him, we will not be fruitful. If we remain connected to him, we will produce much fruit.

The fruit that we followers of Christ produce starts with the fruit of the Holy Spirit, who lives in each Christian. The fruits of the Spirit are love, peace, patience, kindness, righteousness, gentleness, and self-control. These fruits are the result of a life that pleases the Lord. These fruits are internal spiritual attributes that are apparent in our lives and actions as we live and look differently than the world does.

We are called to be in the world but not of the world.

The world would love you as one of its own if you belonged to it, but you are no longer part of the world. I chose you to come out of the world, so it hates you.[2]

We have to stay connected to God if we want the strength to live differently than the world does. As long as we are connected to him, we can draw our strength and nourishment from him (the vine) through the power of the Holy Spirit.

If you pick a flower from the vine, it will live in water for a few days, but then it dies. It doesn't last long. A branch can't survive if it is not connected to its lifeline. But if it is connected to its source of life, (the vine) it is provided all it needs to flourish.

This spring, God put a new desire in my heart. When I told my daughter about it, I first asked her if she were sitting down. I had never enjoyed being outside at all. I had despised lawn work and couldn't have cared less about my yard. But God gave me a desire for flowers, landscaping beds, and my lawn.

I also told one of my best friends, who loves lawn work, and she said, "I knew that."

I said, "What? How?"

She said that God had told her that I would start enjoying lawn work that year. *Wow!*

The vine, the branches, and their connection to God has a whole new meaning to me now and more than ever before. For almost eleven years, I never took care of my lawn. This year, I started watering my plants around my home. As I started watering them, they began doing things that I had not seen them do before. They were alive but not thriving like they would have if I had started many years ago.

We Will Only Survive, Not Thrive, Unless the Creation Is Connected to The Creator.

During this new found desire, I had my plants pruned. Pruning requires cutting back the overgrown and dying parts of the plants, which produces fruitfulness and growth.

Pruning is also a great analogy for our relationship with our vine, Jesus Christ. He prunes, cuts off, and takes back branches or dead things in our lives that are not good for our fruitfulness and growth. This is not comfortable, and sometimes quite painful, but necessary for our good even though we might not understand why. We don't have to understand why. We only need to trust the One who does.

Since I have been caring for my plants and yard, they are starting to look like what they should have all along. It just took me doing my part and caring for the yard in order for that to occur. The difference now is that I am caring for and nourishing the plants so that they not only survive but also thrive.

This lesson can also be applied to our connection with the vine. We need to do our part in our relationship with God by spending time with him, serving, studying the Word of God (the Bible), applying God's Word to our lives, and caring for this earthly and eternal relationship. If we do this in our relationship with our Creator, we, too, will not only survive but also thrive in all that he created us to be. We will be free to be ourselves.

Mature plants and trees have a very strong root structure that enables them to weather the storms. During times of drought, the roots must go deeper into the soil for water. Drought requires a desire to grow and mature.

Similarly, when we weather the storms of life, we will grow and mature if we trust God and *his* will and purpose for these storms. Our roots will grow deeper if we are faithful during the storms of life. We will thrive during these difficult times. When we do this in our lives, the world can't help but notice.

This connection is also important in the body of Christ, the church. We, as children of God, need to be connected to the body of Christ in order to survive and thrive. In 1 Corinthians, Paul writes about the body of Christ:

The human body has many parts, but the many parts make up one whole body. So it is with the body of Christ. Some of us are Jews, some are Gentiles, some are slaves, and some are free. But we have all been baptized into one body by one Spirit, and we all share the same Spirit.

Yes, the body has many different parts, not just one part. If the foot says, "I am not a part of the body because I am not a hand," that does not make it any less a part of the body. And if the ear says, "I am not part of the body because I am not an eye," would that make it any less a part of the body? If the whole body were an eye, how would you hear? Or if your whole body were an ear, how would you smell anything?

But our bodies have many parts, and God has put each part just where he wants it. How strange a body would be if it had only one part! Yes, there are many parts, but only one body. The eye can never say to the hand, "I don't need you." The head can't say to the feet, "I don't need you."

In fact, some parts of the body that seem weakest and least important are actually the most necessary. And the parts we regard as less honorable are those we clothe with the greatest care. So we carefully protect those parts that should not be seen, while the more honorable parts do not require this special care. So God has put the body together such that extra honor and care are given to those parts that have less dignity. This makes for harmony among the members, so that all the members care for each other. If one part suffers, all the parts suffer with it, and if one part is honored, all the parts are glad. All of you together are Christ's body, and each of you is a part of it.[3]

The body of Christ is the church. In order to fulfill the purpose that we were created for, we need to be connected and serving in a local body of believers. Within this local body, we need to develop relationships, use our spiritual gifts, help other members through hard times, love, grow, serve, and so much more.

The church is not just a building. *We* are the church. We are commanded to go into the world and be the hands and feet of Jesus. This is when we make a real eternal impact for the kingdom of God.

Another connection that I want to discuss is between our heads and our hearts. Remember the quote mentioned earlier by Andy Stanley: "Rules without a relationship lead to rebellion"?[4] Let's dissect this a bit, if you will. The "rules" are like head knowledge, and the "relationship" is like the heart knowledge. We must *connect* our heads and hearts in order to have the relationships we need so that we will grow up in our faith and impact others for the kingdom of God.

The Lord said, "I will put my laws in their hearts, and I will write them on their minds."[5] When you have these laws in your heart, you will more than likely also have them in your head. On the contrary, when you put these laws in your mind, a connection does not necessarily take place between your head and heart. There is a greater probability that your heart and head will be connected to God if it begins in the heart.

Here's another story that is an example of the impact we can have when we go into the world as the hands and feet of Jesus. On a week-long mission trip in San Antonio, Texas with high school students from our church's youth group, we were tasked with making repairs to homes of people living below the poverty level.

My group was assigned to a couple who did not know the Lord. They were very sweet and had been through many struggles in their lives. They didn't understand why we would come to their home and help them without getting anything in return. We told them we were helping because we loved Jesus Christ and wanted to help others. In this way, we made Christ known to them through our actions.

As the teens were working on the house, I was able to spend some time with the couple. Throughout the week, God moved in their hearts. On Wednesday, they both gave their lives to Christ. The woman told me that her husband would never have gone to church, but because church had come to them, they gave their lives to Christ.

Now fellow Christians, the work of the church is the reason we remain on earth after being saved. I would not have experienced the results of that mission trip had I not been connected to a local body of believers where I served and taught high school students.

Again, I ask you, what will you choose? Will you be empowered by the Spirit to live connected or enslaved by the flesh to live disconnected? The choice is yours. I pray that after seeing the results of your choice, you will choose to be connected. Your choice will have an earthly and eternal impact.

NOTES

1   John 15: 4 and 5 NLT
2   John 15:19 NLT
3   1 Corinthians 12:12–27 NLT
4   Andy Stanley, "Preaching The Grace of The Law," Sermon Central, November 29, 2010, https://www.sermoncentral.com/pastors-preaching-articles/ andy-stanley -preaching-the-grace-of-the-law-763?ref=PreachingArticleDetails
5   Hebrews 10:16 NLT

CHAPTER 21

Lost Vs Found

The next result of our choice to live in the Spirit or the flesh is being lost versus found. Will you live each day empowered by the Spirit so you can be found or enslaved by the flesh so you will be lost?

The song, "Amazing Grace" says, "I once was lost, but now I am found." We, as children of God, can relate well to these words. We know we were lost in our own ways because we have been found. If you don't realize you are lost, you will have a hard time being found.

We, as children of God, are often referred to as sheep, and Jesus Christ is referred to as our Great Shepherd. This verse in Hebrews says, "Now may the God of peace—who brought up from the dead our Lord Jesus, the great Shepherd of the sheep, and ratified an eternal covenant with his blood"[1]

Another verse in 1 Peter says, "And when the Great Shepherd appears, you will receive a crown of never-ending glory and honor."[2] As our Great Shepherd, he tends us who are his flock. He watches over us, provides for us, protects us, and leads us in the direction he wants us to go to fulfill the perfect will he created for each of us.

When we, as sheep, have a Great Shepherd, we are no longer lost but found. We know who we are (his sheep) and to whom we belong (Jesus Christ).

In Luke 15, Jesus told a story (parable) about the shepherd and his sheep:

If a man has a hundred sheep and one of them gets lost, what will he do? Won't he leave the ninety-nine others in the wilderness and go to search for the one that is lost until he finds it? And when he has found it, he will joyfully carry it home on his shoulders. When he arrives, he will call together his friends and neighbors, saying, "Rejoice with me because I have found my lost sheep." In the same way, there is more joy in heaven over one lost sinner who repents and returns to God than over ninety-nine others who are righteous and haven't strayed away![3]

We, as children of God, should delight in this truth. If we go astray and leave the flock, God will come and find us. Believers, I don't know about you, but it brings me great joy knowing that our Great Shepherd will come and find us if we get lost.

There is similar parable that Jesus told regarding a lost coin in Luke 15:

Or suppose a woman has ten silver coins[a] and loses one. Won't she light a lamp and sweep the entire house and search carefully until she finds it? And when she finds it, she will call in her friends and neighbors and say, "Rejoice with me because I have found my lost coin." In the same way, there is joy in the presence of God's angels when even one sinner repents.[4]

This is another example of how Jesus will look for us until he finds us. Hallelujah!

There is one more parable in which Jesus spoke to us concerning a lost son.

A man had two sons. The younger son told his father, "I want my share of your estate now before you die." So his father agreed to divide his wealth between his sons.

A few days later this younger son packed all his belongings and moved to a distant land, and there he wasted all his money in wild living. About the time his money ran out, a great famine swept over the land, and he began to starve. He persuaded a local farmer to hire him, and the man sent him into his fields to feed the pigs. The young man became so hungry that even the pods he was feeding the pigs looked good to him. But no one gave him anything.

When he finally came to his senses, he said to himself, "At home even the hired servants have food enough to spare, and here I am dying of hunger! I will go home to my father and say, 'Father, I have sinned against both heaven and you, and I am no longer worthy of being called your son. Please take me on as a hired servant.'"

So he returned home to his father. And while he was still a long way off, his father saw him coming. Filled with love and compassion, he ran to his son, embraced him, and kissed him. His son said to him, "Father, I have sinned against both heaven and you, and I am no longer worthy of being called your son."

But his father said to the servants, "Quick! Bring the finest robe in the house and put it on him. Get a ring for his finger and sandals for his feet. And kill the calf we have been fattening. We must celebrate with a feast, for this son of mine was dead and has now returned to life. He was lost, but now he is found." So the party began.

Meanwhile, the older son was in the fields working. When he returned home, he heard music and dancing in the house, and he asked one of the servants what was going on. "Your brother is back," he was told, "and your father has killed the fattened calf. We are celebrating because of his safe return."

The older brother was angry and wouldn't go in. His father came out and begged him, but he replied, "All these years I've slaved for you and never once refused to do a single thing you told me to. And in all that time you never gave me even one young goat for a feast with my friends. Yet when this son of yours comes back after squandering your money on prostitutes, you celebrate by killing the fattened calf!"

His father said to him, "Look, dear son, you have always stayed by me, and everything I have is yours. We had to celebrate this happy day. For your brother was dead and has come back to life! He was lost, but now he is found!"[5]

When we are lost, Jesus Christ will come and find us. When we return to the flock, there will be great celebration on earth and in heaven.

The next passage of scripture talks about wandering away from God: "I have wandered away like a lost sheep; come and find me, for I have not forgotten your commands."[6] Also, "My people have been lost sheep. Their shepherds have led them astray and turned them loose in the mountains. They have lost their way and can't remember how to get back to the sheepfold."[7] This passage speaks about false teachers in the world who tell lies, and through them, we can be led astray. We must know the truth (the Word of God or the Holy Bible) in order to determine if what others say agrees with what God says.

Lastly, the scripture says, "Household gods give worthless advice, fortune-tellers predict only lies, and interpreters of dreams pronounce falsehoods that give no comfort. So my people are wandering like lost sheep; they are attacked because they have no shepherd."[8] This verse tells us what can happen if we don't have a shepherd: We will be "wandering like lost sheep." We, the sheep, need a shepherd.

Sheep are meek, gentle, and quiet animals who need to be in a flock with a trusted shepherd and to distance themselves from the world. This is how we should live. Through a close relationship with Jesus Christ, our Great Shepherd, we will have all that we need to make it in this world, to make a difference in the world, and to find the way to eternal paradise.

King David wrote about our need for a shepherd and all that the shepherd does for us.

The Lord is my shepherd; I have all that I need. He lets me rest in green meadows; he leads me beside peaceful streams. He renews my strength. He guides me along right paths, bringing honor to his name. Even when I walk through the darkest valley, I will not be afraid, for you are close beside me. Your rod and your staff protect and comfort me. You prepare a feast for me in the presence of my enemies. You honor me by anointing my head with oil. My cup overflows with blessings. Surely your goodness and unfailing love will pursue me all the days of my life, and I will live in the house of the Lord forever.[9]

We are lost and can't find our way through life without Jesus Christ. It is not our way but his that we need. When we choose his way of life, it will be a life of abundance and fulfillment as we do his perfect will for our lives. We find real life when we are truly found.

Again I ask you, what will you choose? Will you live empowered by the Spirit to be found or enslaved by the flesh to be lost? The choice is yours. I pray after seeing the results of your choice, you will choose to be found. Your choice will have an earthly and eternal impact.

NOTES

1   Hebrews 13:20 NLT
2   1 Peter 5:4 NLT
3   Luke 15:4–7 NLT
4   Luke 15: 8–10 NLT
5   Luke 15:11–32 NLT
6   Psalm 119:176 NLT
7   Jeremiah 50:6 NLT
8   Zechariah 10:2 NLT
9   Psalm 23 NLT

CHAPTER 22

Old Vs New

The next result of our choice to live in the Spirit or in the flesh is living old versus living new. Are you going to be empowered each day by the Spirit to live new or enslaved by the flesh to live old?

This first passage of scripture talks about how we have a "new" life with Christ: "That is what the Scriptures mean when God told him, 'I have made you the father of many nations.' This happened because Abraham believed in the God who brings the dead back to life and who creates new things out of nothing."[1] Did you catch the phrase, "new things out of nothing"? Praise God, because I was certainly less than nothing before I found Christ.

This next passage says, "Yes, Adam's one sin brings condemnation for everyone, but Christ's one act of righteousness brings a right relationship with God and new life for everyone."[2] The act of righteousness by Christ was his death on the cross for our sins, his taking our punishment, and his paying the debt in full once and for all. Hallelujah!

This *new life* is explained very well in Romans: "But now we have been released from the law, for we died to it and are no longer captive to its power. Now we can serve God, not in the old way of obeying the letter of the law, but in the new way of living in the Spirit."[3] This is the key to living a life that is pleasing to God: relying on the Holy Spirit's power, which has come to all post-resurrection believers.

We are post-resurrection believers who have the power of the Holy Spirit in us. But are we reaping the full benefits of this gift?

One of my favorite verses in the Bible is this one: "This means that anyone who belongs to Christ has become a new person. The old life is gone; a new life has begun!"[4] This verse rings true for me and many other followers of Jesus Christ. Since I gave my life to Jesus Christ, it has not been the same. I don't desire my old ways but do desire new ways. These *new* ways are of Christ, and are righteous, pure, and holy. As you feed these new desires, the old desires fade away.

In Romans we read: "Do not let any part of your body become an instrument of evil to serve sin. Instead, give yourselves completely to God, for you were dead, but now you have new life. So use your whole body as an instrument to do what is right for the glory of God."[5] In your *new life*, you will be used by God to do right and to give him the glory.

Another passage in Romans says, "Don't copy the behavior and customs of this world, but let God transform you into a new person by changing the way you think. Then you will learn to know God's will for you, which is good and pleasing and perfect."[6] This is a powerful truth: Thoughts lead to actions, which lead to habits, which lead to behaviors, which lead to attitudes. It all starts in our minds. God can transform us by changing our way of thinking.

The next passage speaks about how our *new person* is to become more like Christ. In Ephesians, we read: "Put on your new nature, created to be like God—truly righteous and holy."[7] In addition, "Put on your new nature, and be renewed as you learn to know your Creator and become like him."[8]

We need to focus our new selves on knowing our Creator, God, and becoming more like him. This is known as sanctification.

We can't have a healthy relationship unless we have trust. This passage focuses on trust in our relationship with God: "For you were buried with Christ when you were baptized. And with him you were raised to new life because you trusted the mighty power of God, who raised Christ from the dead."[9] Our new life with Christ is only possible when we trust God and his power to make us new through the power of the Holy Spirit.

Again I ask you, what will you choose? Will you be empowered by the Spirit to live a new life or enslaved by the flesh to an old life? The choice is yours. I pray that after seeing the results of your choice, you will choose to be new. Your choice will have an earthly and eternal impact.

NOTES

1   Romans 4:17 NLT
2   Romans 5:18 NLT
3   Romans 7:6 NLT
4   2 Corinthians 5:17 NLT
5   Romans 6:13 NLT
6   Romans 12:2 NLT
7   Ephesians 4:24 NLT
8   Colossians 3:10 NLT
9   Colossians 2:12 NLT

CHAPTER 23

Fearful Vs Fearless

The next result of our choice to be in the Spirit or in the flesh is living fearfully versus fearlessly. Are you going to be empowered each day by the Spirit to live fearlessly or enslaved by the flesh to live fearfully?

This verse tells how God will be with us in our fears: "So do not fear, for I am with you; do not be dismayed, for I am your God. I will strengthen you and help you; I will uphold you with my righteous right hand."[1] God is with us. If we have the omnipotent (all-powerful) God with us, we should not fear. He will give us help and strength to get through times when we are afraid.

Here is another passage of scripture in which we learn that God is with us during fearful times: "Have I not commanded you? Be strong and courageous. Do not be terrified; do not be discouraged, for the Lord your God will be with you wherever you go."[2] This next passage also tells us to be strong and courageous: "Be strong and courageous. Do not be afraid or terrified because of them, for the Lord your God goes with you; he will never leave you nor forsake you."[3]

This passage paints a beautiful mental picture of what a child of God looks like in the spiritual world: "The angel of the Lord encamps around those who fear him, and he delivers them."[4] Encamps also means to settle in. That is a great truth to hold on to during times of fear. The Lord and his angels are settled within us, and they will never leave us.

In Psalms, we discover another reason not to fear: "The Lord is for me, so I will have no fear. What can mere people do to me?"[5] When God is for us, we can live without fear. In Romans, we read: "What shall we say about such wonderful things as these? If God is for us, who can ever be against us?"[6] Along this same vein, in Hebrews, we read: "So we can say with confidence, 'The Lord is my helper, so I will have no fear. What can mere people do to me?' "[7]

Another passage says, "For I am the Lord, your God, who takes hold of your right hand and says to you, 'Do not fear; I will help you."[8] The Lord will not only help us but will fight for us:

Do not be afraid of them; the Lord your God himself will fight for you.[9] No one can stand against God!

When God is for and with us, we can live without fear. When overcoming fear, we need to trust God completely.

See, God has come to save me. I will trust in him and not be afraid. The Lord God is my strength and my song; he has given me victory.[10]

Another verse on trust says, "When I am afraid, I put my trust in you."[11] When we trust in the Lord, he can overcome all of our fears. We get strength from the Lord and are given victory over life and death. If God sent his only Son to die for our sins, would he not save us, those for whom he paid the ultimate price of his Son's death? We can trust him.

When we believe someone, we trust that person.

Jesus told him, "Don't be afraid; just believe."[12]

We can believe Jesus more than anyone or anything else in our lives. He is *all* righteousness and goodness. He is completely trustworthy. No one or nothing can compare to God.

In Proverbs, King Solomon talked about fear within the context of common sense and discernment:

My child, don't lose sight of common sense and discernment. Hang on to them, for they will refresh your soul. They are like jewels on a necklace. They keep you safe on your way, and your feet will not stumble. You can go to bed without fear; you will lie down and sleep soundly. You need not be afraid of sudden disaster or the destruction that comes upon the wicked, for the Lord is your security. He will keep your foot from being caught in a trap.[13]

God gives us common sense and discernment, which refresh our souls. I am living proof that there is no fear for those who are in Christ Jesus. The Lord is our security. We don't need to be afraid of disaster or destruction because we are not wicked but are children of God.

King David wrote in Psalm 27, "The Lord is my light and my salvation—whom shall I fear? The Lord is the stronghold of my life—of whom shall I be afraid?"[14] Fear can be a darkness that imprisons us and keeps us from being all that God created us to be. The Lord is the antidote to that darkness because of his glorious light. He is also the stronghold (a place of refuge and security) of our lives.

Jesus said, "Peace I leave with you; my peace I give you. I do not give to you as the world gives. Do not let your hearts be troubled and do not be afraid."[15] This peace is not based on circumstances but is a confident assurance from the Holy Spirit. This peace, unlike the peace in this world, gives us a reason to have no fear of the present or the future.

This next verse also tells us what God provides for his children through the Holy Spirit: "For God has not given us a spirit of fear and timidity, but of power, love, and self-discipline."[16] Did you get that? God does not give us fear, but our enemy does. God gives us power, love, and a sound mind, which are great characteristics of a strong spiritual leader. We can choose to let the enemy win the battle over our effectiveness in our Christian lives, or we can believe what God says he provides through the help of the Holy Spirit.

This verse is a powerful antidote for fear: "There is no fear in love. But perfect love drives out fear, because fear has to do with punishment. The one who fears is not made perfect in love."[17] God's perfect, unfailing love for us is a powerful truth and a way that we can overcome our fears. There is no punishment for God's children because our sins have been paid for by the blood of Jesus Christ.

So now there is no condemnation for those who belong to Christ Jesus.[18]

We, as children of God, can live without fear, unlike the wicked who are headed for death and destruction. They will have to pay their own punishment for eternity, unless they give their lives to Jesus Christ, who will forgive them by his blood.

Because we have been forgiven, we can live as this verse says: "Tell everyone who is discouraged, Be strong and don't be afraid! God is coming to your rescue, coming to punish your enemies."[19] We can live without fear now and with hope for future eternal deliverance from all sin and evil.

This is also an important passage of scripture to look at when discussing fear: "Make the Lord of Heaven's Armies holy in your life. He is the one you should fear. He is the one who should make you tremble. He will keep you safe."[20] Fear of the Lord doesn't mean that we are literally scared of him, but that we revere him and his Word like we revere our parents or family members who love us and are looking out for our best. Fearing the Lord can also be fearing his wrath and judgment if we don't know him and we are not his children.

In reference to the fear of God, King Solomon said in Proverbs, "Fear of the Lord is the foundation of wisdom. Knowledge of the Holy One results in good judgment."[21] If fearing the Lord is the underlying principle of wisdom, then that is the foundation on which we should build our lives.

The last but often best method to drive out fear is prayer.

I prayed to the Lord, and he answered me. He freed me from all my fears.[22]

Prayer is direct communication with God. We ask him, and he answers. God always answers our prayers. However, it happens on God's time and not on our time. It is not always the answer we want. It might be yes, no, maybe, or wait. We might not understand the answer, but we know the One who does and trust him with every detail of our lives.

I know firsthand about fear because of my childhood experiences. As I mentioned earlier, my daddy was an alcoholic who physically abused my mother. Every day I lived in fear of my daddy's wrath toward my mom, whom I loved. I didn't want her to get hurt. Many times I would stand in the gap between my mom and dad because I knew he wouldn't hit me. This fear imprisoned me, and I could find no safe, secure environment in which to be a child.

Other fears stemmed from my mother's upbringing. Born into a wealthy family, she said someone was always trying to break into her childhood home. She developed a fear that she never got over, and we learned that fear from her.

When my daddy travelled, my mother made us all sleep in her bed. She locked the bedroom door, and awoke at every sound. After she left my dad and was living alone, she never lived in any place except a high-rise building because that way, no one could break into her apartment through the windows. Fear imprisoned her all of her life.

The only antidote to my mother's fear was to know the one who could deliver her from fear—Jesus Christ. But she didn't know these truths that we are discussing in this book, and that makes my heart heavy.

Thankfully, I know how it feels to be released from fear. Since I accepted Jesus Christ I have been released from fear because I have God as my constant companion. He protects me and has assigned guardian angels to me and all of his children. The enemy sees us with a hedge of protection surrounding us and the blood of Christ over us. Now isn't this the safest and most secure place we could ever be? Then why do we still fear?

Satan and his fallen angels have to get God's permission to attack us, as in the story of Job. God allows these attacks in our lives as he did in Job's to test us to see if we will be faithful and trust him in the good and bad times. But God is with us all the way. He equips us with all that we need to pass each test. Doesn't this give us the freedom to live fearless?

Again I ask you what will you choose? Will you be empowered by the Spirit to live fearlessly or enslaved by the flesh to live fearfully? The choice is yours. I pray that after seeing the results of your choice, you will choose to be fearless. Your choice will have an earthly and eternal impact.

NOTES

1   Isaiah 41:10 NIV
2   Joshua 1:9 NIV
3   Deuteronomy 31:6 NIV
4   Psalm 34:7 NIV
5   Psalm 118:6 NLT
6   Romans 8:31NLT
7   Hebrews 13:6 NLT
8   Isaiah 41:13 NIV
9   Deuteronomy 3:22 NIV
10 Isaiah 12:2 NLT
11 Psalm 56:3 NLT
12 Mark 5:36 NIV
13 Proverbs 3:21–26 NLT
14 Psalm 27:1 NIV
15 John 14:27 NIV
16 2 Timothy 1:7 NLT
17 1 John 4:18 NIV
18 Romans 8:1 NLT
19 Isaiah 35:4 NLT
20 Isaiah 8:13 and 14 NLT
21 Proverbs 9:10 NLT
22 Psalm 34:4 NLT

CHAPTER 24

Strength Vs Weakness

The next result of our choice to be in the Spirit or in the flesh is living with strength versus weakness. Will you be empowered each day by the Spirit to live with strength or enslaved by the flesh to live in weakness?

The apostle Paul said, "For I can do everything through Christ, who gives me strength."[1] This is one of the most quoted verses in the Bible. Through Jesus Christ, we have the strength to do everything. This beautiful verse tells us how God equips his children with the strength that we need to accomplish everything he created us to do to impact his kingdom and give him glory.

We are not superhumans who have the strength to do everything on our own, but through Jesus Christ we have strength. We are going to be *all* that God created us to be so that we can fulfill His perfect will. When we are living within his perfect will, we will have the strength we need to get through the good and the bad times. We don't have this strength when we have not accepted Jesus Christ into our lives and are living outside of his perfect will in unrepentant, habitual patterns of sin. We are left on our own when we are living this way. That is a scary place to be.

Now that we have looked at how we can do everything through Christ who gives us the strength, let's look at another verse the apostle Paul wrote: "Each time he said, 'My grace is all you need. My power works best in weakness.' So now I am glad to boast about my weaknesses, so that the power of Christ can work through me. That's why I take pleasure in my weaknesses, and in the insults, hardships, persecutions, and troubles that

I suffer for Christ. For when I am weak, then I am strong."[2] This is a very powerful verse and counterintuitive to the world's views.

When we are weak, then we are strong. If God reveals himself through our weaknesses, we should reveal our areas of weakness so that God will be able to reveal his strengths through them and get the glory for them.

I have many cracks—areas of weakness—in my clay pot from sex, alcohol, drugs, pride, money, success, abortions, codependency, and more, which God can use for his glory. If I hide my cracks, God can't use them in my life or in the lives of others. We experience freedom when we reveal our cracks to others and help them see how God has used our cracks to help us. There is so much freedom when we have transparency in our lives. Let the light within us shine through our cracks, our weaknesses.

I have been teaching in the high school student ministry at my local church for over ten years. I can tell you that I have had the greatest impact when I have revealed my struggles or cracks. The students know that I show up each week having made a mess of my life on my own. They also know that God has taken my mess and turned it into a message for him and his glory. That's how God works in our weaknesses to reveal his strengths.

The apostle Paul wrote about boasting in this verse: "If I must boast, I would rather boast about the things that show how weak I am."[3] When we boast about how weak we are, it helps others relate to us.

If we all are truthful in our self-reflection, we know we have weaknesses. If we have trouble admitting or exposing them, we need to check ourselves. People who don't know the Lord usually don't have the strength to admit their weaknesses. But as children of God who have been redeemed by Jesus Christ, we need to reveal our weaknesses to others. In doing this, they will recognize God in our humble weaknesses, and seeds will be planted in the hearts of nonbelievers. This is different from what nonbelievers do. We are called to be different because in that difference, others will come to know him.

In that same vein, Paul said this: "When I am with those who are weak, I share their weakness, for I want to bring the weak to Christ. Yes, I try to find common ground with everyone, doing everything I can to save some."[4] When we find common ground with others, they will be able to relate to us and know that we have struggled through the same things.

What better way to relate to someone who is going through a hard time than someone who has already traveled that same road. Because of this common ground, you can share how you managed this tough road and how Jesus Christ was the only one who could smooth things out for you.

Do you know who else has common ground with us? Jesus Christ does. Look at this verse: "This High Priest of ours understands our weaknesses, for he faced all of the same testings we do, yet he did not sin."[5] Jesus Christ experienced tough roads in his life here on earth yet didn't sin. One of the reasons he came to earth in human form was so that he could relate to our tough roads by traveling them himself.

In this next passage, we learn more about how powerful God is and how his power works in and through us: "Although he was crucified in weakness, he now lives by the power of God. We, too, are weak, just as Christ was, but when we deal with you we will be alive with him and will have God's power."[6] We can have God's power in our lives. The more we know and trust him, the more power we will have that can be used to impact God's kingdom on earth and for eternity.

A verse in Isaiah says, "He gives power to the weak and strength to the powerless."[7] Remember, it is in our weakness that he can reveal his strength. When God reveals his power and strength in and through us, our job is to recognize the power is from God and to give him the glory.

In 1 Corinthians we read: "This foolish plan of God is wiser than the wisest of human plans, and God's weakness is stronger than the greatest of human strength."[8] God is wiser and stronger than the wisest and strongest human. We are confined to our flesh, which is finite and temporary. God is infinite, omnipotent, omnipresent, and omniscient. God is indescribable. There is no comparison between God and us. He is the great I Am. Who are we with our finite minds to attempt to comprehend an infinite God.

Yet he became human because of his unfailing love for us. He gives us all that we want and need of him to help us in our lives and in the lives of others. His unfailing love for us is something we can't comprehend, but we can trust him and his character. In fact, one of the two greatest commandments that Jesus gave was, "And you must love the Lord your God with all your heart, all your soul, all your mind, and all your strength."[9]

God wants *all* of us and not just part of us. If God is not first and the only one or thing in that premier spot, then he doesn't have all of us. We should not compartmentalize God because if we do, he is not first and only a part of us. We are shortchanging ourselves if we don't give God all of us because we will miss out on the abundant life that Jesus promised us.

We, as current-day Christians, are following in the footsteps of the Israelites as they left Egypt. They wandered in the desert for forty years. We who haven't given all of ourselves to God are also wandering and not living the abundant life that Jesus came to provide for us (the promised land).

Again I ask you, what will you choose? Will you be empowered by the Spirit to live strongly or enslaved by the flesh to live weakly? The choice is yours. I pray after seeing the results of your choice, you will choose to be strong. Your choice will have an earthly and eternal impact.

NOTES

1   Philippians 4:13 NLT
2   2 Corinthians 12:9 and 10 NLT
3   2 Corinthians 11:30 NLT
4   1 Corinthians 9:22 NLT
5   Hebrews 4:15 NLT
6   2 Corinthians 13:4 NLT
7   Isaiah 40:29 NLT
8   1 Corinthians 1:25 NLT
9   Mark 12:30 NLT

CHAPTER 25

Generous Vs Greedy

The next result of our choice to live in the Spirit or in the flesh is being generous versus being greedy. Are you going to live each day empowered by the Spirit to be generous or enslaved by the flesh to be greedy?

First, being generous is a spiritual gift. What does this mean? Spiritual gifts are given to us when we become children of God, we accept Jesus Christ into our hearts, and the Holy Spirit comes to dwell within us. The Bible talks about spiritual gifts in the following passage of scripture:

In his grace, God has given us different gifts for doing certain things well. So if God has given you the ability to prophesy, speak out with as much faith as God has given you. If your gift is serving others, serve them well. If you are a teacher, teach well. If your gift is to encourage others, be encouraging. If it is giving, give generously. If God has given you leadership ability, take the responsibility seriously. And if you have a gift for showing kindness to others, do it gladly.[1]

So giving is a gift from the Spirit. Now you might be thinking, *That gets me out of having to give since it is not my spiritual gift.* Well, that is wrong. We are to be Christ-like, and Jesus was generous with everyone and regarded other people's needs above his own. All we have and all that is on earth is God's anyway. He has just given us some of his stuff while we are here on earth.

We are so absorbed with obtaining more and more, but life is just a temporary experience and not our home. We can't take anything we have here to heaven, so why do we focus so much time and energy on getting more money and things during our lives. It is because our flesh is never satisfied and will never get enough. Again, God created us this way so that we will keep searching until we find him.

Jesus said it this way: "Don't store up treasures here on earth, where moths eat them and rust destroys them, and where thieves break in and steal. Store your treasures in heaven, where moths and rust cannot destroy, and thieves do not break in and steal. Wherever your treasure is, there the desires of your heart will also be."[2] We should be more focused on our heavenly treasures than our earthly ones. The true treasure and desire of our hearts should be an intimate relationship with Jesus Christ, being his representatives here on earth, and revealing him to those who don't know him. By living this way, we will store up eternal, heavenly treasures that can't be taken away and that we will be able to enjoy eternally.

The apostle Paul said in Acts, "And I have been a constant example of how you can help those in need by working hard. You should remember the words of the Lord Jesus: 'It is more blessed to give than to receive.' "[3] We need to do the same things that Paul did in his life. As Christ-like examples, we need to give more than we receive. In return, we will be blessed more. God knows the motives of our hearts, and he will only bless us if we have the right intent.

In Luke, Jesus said, "Give, and you will receive. Your gift will return to you in full—pressed down, shaken together to make room for more, running over, and poured into your lap. The amount you give will determine the amount you get back."[4] We need to follow this truth in our lives. Again, we must check that our motives are not for selfish gain. Giving will be noticed by others. They will see something different in us and want what we have—Jesus Christ.

Luke also wrote about giving in these verses:

While Jesus was in the Temple, he watched the rich people dropping their gifts in the collection box. Then a poor widow came by and dropped in two small coins. "I tell you the truth," Jesus said, "this poor widow has given more than all the rest of them. For they have given a tiny part of their surplus, but she, poor as she is, has given everything she has."[5]

This widow gave all that she had although she had few resources to make money. But we, like most, give a tiny part of our surplus. She must have had great faith to trust that God would provide for her. Is our faith that strong?

Solomon wrote about generosity in several places throughout the book of Proverbs. When King Solomon was granted one wish from God, he asked for wisdom. So these verses are from the wisdom that was given to him from God.

Give freely and become more wealthy; be stingy and lose everything. The generous will prosper; those who refresh others will themselves be refreshed.[6]

When we are generous with what we have, it releases us from the enslavement of our possessions and puts things in the right perspective that everything is God's anyway. We are just using them temporarily.

Solomon also wrote many verses in Proverbs about helping the poor:

If you help the poor, you are lending to the Lord—and he will repay you![7]

Blessed are those who are generous, because they feed the poor.[8]

Those who shut their ears to the cries of the poor will be ignored in their own time of need.[9]

It is a sin to belittle one's neighbor; blessed are those who help the poor.[10]

Whoever gives to the poor will lack nothing, but those who close their eyes to poverty will be cursed.[11]

We should not dismiss Solomon's words. Helping the poor is a way to show others the hands and feet of Jesus. Since we do not help others in order to be repaid, people will wonder why we are helping. Therefore, we can reveal to them that our compassion comes from the Lord and help them understand how much Jesus loves each of them.

If someone has enough money to live well and sees a brother or sister in need but shows no compassion—how can God's love be in that person?[12]

In 1 Timothy, Paul wrote to the young spiritual leader Timothy about giving.

Teach those who are rich in this world not to be proud and not to trust in their money, which is so unreliable. Their trust should be in God, who richly gives us all we need for our enjoyment. Tell them to use their money to do good. They should be rich in good works and generous to those in need, always being ready to share with others. By doing this they will be storing up their treasure as a good foundation for the future so that they may experience true life.[13]

God provides us with all we need for our enjoyment and for experiencing true life. Money—or anything else the world has to offer—doesn't provide that for us. We can't serve two masters: money and God. Money can't buy true life. The only way to find true life is to find God and to have a close personal relationship with him through his Son, Jesus Christ.

Paul also wrote to the church in Corinth regarding giving: "You must each decide in your heart how much to give. And don't give reluctantly or in response to pressure. For God loves a person who gives cheerfully. And God will generously provide all you need. Then you will always have everything you need and plenty left over to share with others."[14]

The amount you give is not as important as the attitude you have toward giving.

Give generously to the poor, not grudgingly, for the Lord your God will bless you in everything you do.[15]

In Matthew, Jesus spoke about giving to the needy:

Watch out! Don't do your good deeds publicly, to be admired by others, for you will lose the reward from your Father in heaven. When you give to someone in need, don't do as the hypocrites do—blowing trumpets in the synagogues and streets to call attention to their acts of charity! I tell you the truth, they have received all the reward they will ever get. But when you give to someone in need, don't let your left hand know what your right hand is doing. Give your gifts in private, and your Father, who sees everything, will reward you.[16]

When we give with the right motives, only God needs to know. Secret giving and other random acts of kindness reap more eternal rewards because there is no earthly recognition. The motive of our hearts should be to give God all the glory and not to bring glory to ourselves.

In Proverbs we read this: "Honor the Lord with your wealth and with the best part of everything you produce. Then he will fill your barns with grain, and your vats will overflow with good wine."[17] We are instructed to give God the first, best fruits from our labors and not our leftovers. When we do this, we demonstrate that God, and not our money and possessions, has first place in our lives. We show that *all* belongs to him and so do we.

In the book of Malachi we find the one area in which God says we may put him to the test: " 'Bring all the tithes into the storehouse so there will be enough food in my Temple. If you do,' says the Lord of Heaven's Armies, 'I will open the windows of heaven for you. I will pour out a blessing so great you won't have enough room to take it in! Try it! Put me to the test!' "[18] We are commanded to tithe from the first and best fruits of our labor, and when we do, God will overflow our storehouses. We may test him on this. Sometimes, our *storehouses* are overflowing with blessings that are not money or possessions, but are internal attributes that are priceless and that nonbelievers don't have. Because of these internal blessings, we are different from the inside out, and others in the world will notice it.

Lastly, I want to discuss one other verse on generosity. In Matthew, we read: "And the King will say, 'I tell you the truth, when you did it to one of the least of these my brothers and sisters, you were doing it to me!' "[19] When we give to the most vulnerable in our world—the orphans, widows, and the poor—with the right motives and looking for nothing in return, we glorify God.

Again I ask you, what will you choose? Will you live empowered by the Spirit to be generous or enslaved by the flesh to be greedy? The choice is yours. I pray that after seeing the results of your choice, you will choose to be generous. Your choice will have an earthly and eternal impact.

NOTES

1   Romans 12: 6–8 NLT
2   Matthew 6:19–21 NLT
3   Acts 20:35 NLT
4   Luke 6:38 NLT
5   Luke 21:1–4 NLT
6   Proverbs 11:24–25 NLT
7   Proverbs 19:17 NLT
8   Proverbs 22:9 NLT
9   Proverbs 21:13 NLT
10   Proverbs 14:21 NLT
11   Proverbs 28:27 NLT
12   1 John 3:17 NLT
13   1 Timothy 6:17–19 NLT
14   2 Corinthians 9:7–8 NLT
15   Deuteronomy 15:10 NLT
16   Matthew 6:1–4 NLT
17   Proverbs 3:9–10 NLT
18   Malachi 3:10 NLT
19   Matthew 25:40 NLT

CHAPTER 26

Innocent Vs Guilty

The next result of our choice to live in the Spirit or in the flesh is being innocent versus guilty. Will you live each day empowered by the Spirit to be innocent or enslaved by the flesh to be guilty?

Let's discuss the beginning of human life with Adam and Eve in the garden of Eden. When Adam and Eve sinned against God, they caused sin to enter human nature. Because we are all descendants of Adam and Eve, we are all infected with the seed of sin. We are all born sinners with sinful natures that dwell in each of us.

As we discussed earlier in the book, God had a plan to bring us back to himself through his Son, Jesus Christ. Through the sacrifice of Jesus, we can be forgiven from all of our sins, past, present, and future. This forgiveness is available to all of us, and it is what we need more than the next breath we take. You see, we were not created to be able to bear the burden of our sins. When we try to bear that burden, our lives fill with turmoil and dissatisfaction.

This verse in Romans is a freeing one for those who have accepted the forgiveness that only Jesus Christ can bring: "So now there is no condemnation for those who belong to Christ Jesus."[1] Do you understand this? There is no condemnation—blame, judgment, disappointment, sentencing, conviction—for us who belong to Jesus Christ. We are innocent of our sins. The punishment has been paid in full by the sacrifice of Christ on the cross.

Now that we have established how we can live without the guilt that we so rightly deserve, we need to be careful not to judge others.

Do not judge others, and you will not be judged.[2]

Do not condemn others, or it will all come back against you. Forgive others, and you will be forgiven[3]

We must approach everyone on earth in this way. Because people of the world do not live this way, we can show our difference in powerful ways by not judging or condemning, but by forgiving others. When we forgive others, it is not because they deserve to be forgiven. No one does. Forgiveness is for you and me. It helps to release us from harboring bitterness and anger that continues to brew inside of us and not in them, when we are not forgiving. Forgiveness allows us to move forward in freedom from harboring unforgiveness.

We have a very hard time finding fault with ourselves, but we can easily point out the faults of others. The Bible says, "People may be right in their own eyes, but the Lord examines their heart."[4] The Lord knows our hearts and our innermost motives. Nothing can be hidden from him. We might be right in our own opinion, but our hearts may tell a different story. We should not judge others so that we won't be judged. We are all flawed humans created by a flawless God.

Another verse that goes along with our lack of ability to self-assess our own lives, says it this way: "Hypocrite! First get rid of the log in your own eye; then you will see well enough to deal with the speck in your friend's eye."[5] It is easy for us humans to look at the problems of others but not to accept and address our own. Until we look at ourselves and deal with our own issues, we certainly can't have the right mind-set and eye sight to see others.

We, as believers, are hypocritical when we judge not only nonbelievers but also other believers in Christ, who are our own brothers and sisters.

So why do you condemn another believer? Why do you look down on another believer? Remember, we will all stand before the judgment seat of God. For the Scriptures say, "As surely as I live," says the Lord, "every knee will bend to me, and every tongue will declare allegiance to God." Yes, each of us will give a personal account to God. So let's stop condemning each other. Decide instead to live in such a way that you will not cause another believer to stumble and fall.[6]

We should not judge anyone else because we will *all* stand in front of the throne of God and be rewarded or punished according to how we lived our lives while on earth.

So don't make judgments about anyone ahead of time—before the Lord returns. For he will bring our darkest secrets to light and will reveal our private motives. Then God will give to each one whatever praise is due.[7]

In the end times, *everyone* will bow down to God and confess that Jesus Christ is Lord. We can either get on board with God through Jesus Christ now or be forced to later. The consequences of our decision will have an eternal impact. Once Jesus Christ comes again, it will be too late to change our minds.

Let's now look at what it is like if we don't accept the forgiveness offered only through the blood that was shed by Jesus Christ on the cross.

For the wages of sin is death, but the free gift of God is eternal life through Christ Jesus our Lord.[8]

If we are going to pay the price for our own sins, it will end in death. This death is not only a physical death but more importantly a spiritual death. The impact of this decision, that only we can make for ourselves and for no one else, will affect us while here on earth and for eternity.

What will it be like when Jesus comes back to earth for the second coming? I wanted to share my personal vision of what this might be like with you. Please realize that I, a finite, fleshly, sinful-natured being, can't even begin to comprehend what God has planned for that day.

I picture that we will all be caught up in the clouds, will see God on his throne, and see Jesus Christ at his right hand. We can't survive the sight of God or Jesus while we are still in our fleshly state, so our fleshly bodies are left behind. We will have our souls and new spiritual bodies there. We will each approach the throne of God and give a personal account to God of our life on earth. We believers in Jesus Christ, who have accepted Jesus and the forgiveness of our sins, have Jesus Christ as our attorney. The devil will be the attorney who is against us.

The devil, will try to tattle on us, but Jesus will shut him down and say to God, the Judge, that our debt has been paid in full. All of our sins have been paid for, and God doesn't even remember them at all.

He has removed our sins as far from us as the east is from the west.[9]

God will reward our lives, not because of what we have done but because of what Jesus did for us. We will enter heaven and live eternally with him in paradise.

No eye has seen, no ear has heard, and no mind has imagined what God has prepared for those who love him.[10]

Hallelujah!

Those who did not accept Jesus Christ and his forgiveness of their sins will have a situation like this: "But all who reject me and my message will be judged on the day of judgment by the truth I have spoken."[11] They will approach the throne of God and will give a personal account of their lives. Their attorney will be the devil. Jesus will be the attorney against them. The devil will begin to lay out all of their sins before the whole world that they have committed while on earth. This won't be a private meeting in the judge's court, but it will be broadcasted for the world to see.

After the devil lays out his case *against* them, even though he is supposed to be working *for* them, Jesus will say that they are guilty as charged. They will then be punished for *all* that they have done and will be sentenced to hell to pay for all of their wrongs. Someone has to pay the price for our sins. If we don't accept Jesus Christ, the only one who can pay the price is us. *Ouch!*

For we must all stand before Christ to be judged. We will each receive whatever we deserve for the good or evil we have done in this earthly body.[12]

God will judge all the earth with righteousness.

Let the rivers clap their hands in glee! Let the hills sing out their songs of joy before the Lord, for he is coming to judge the earth. He will judge the world with justice, and the nations with fairness.[13]

The Bible also talks about God's judgment in this next passage: "And remember that the heavenly Father to whom you pray has no favorites. He will judge or reward you according to what you do. So you must live in reverent fear of him during your time here as 'temporary residents.' "[14] God has no favorites, and everyone, regardless of what he or she has done, can come to God and receive forgiveness through his Son, Jesus Christ.

If we have a relationship with God through Jesus Christ, we have nothing to fear when the day of judgment comes.

And as we live in God, our love grows more perfect. So we will not be afraid on the day of judgment, but we can face him with confidence because we live like Jesus here in this world.[15]

We are called to become more like Christ (sanctification) during our temporary residency here on earth. In our sanctification process, we will live more like Jesus and bring others to know him because we are different from the world.

The Lord is coming back soon.

Look, I am coming soon, bringing my reward with me to repay all people according to their deeds.[16]

This should motivate us to do what is right and be bold about our faith so that others won't have to suffer eternally from the consequences of their sins.

For those who say he is not coming back, this verse is a great way to explain why he has not come back yet: "The Lord isn't really being slow about his promise, as some people think. No, he is being patient for your sake. He does not want anyone to be destroyed, but wants everyone to repent."[17] God loves each of us so much that he doesn't want anyone to be separated from him. He wants all of us to repent before it is too late. He created and loves us with an unfailing love, which we can't comprehend.

He will come again. The first time he destroyed the earth with water. The next time it will be destroyed by fire.

Then he used the water to destroy the ancient world with a mighty flood. And by the same word, the present heavens and earth have been stored up for fire. They are being kept for the day of judgment, when ungodly people will be destroyed.[18]

Judgment by fire can be found in this verse as well: "He will come with his mighty angels, in flaming fire, bringing judgment on those who don't know God and on those who refuse to obey the Good News of our Lord Jesus."[19] This is what some people are talking about when they say, "Turn or burn." They are telling you to repent of your sins or to face the judgment by fire upon the Lord's second coming.

Now, let me ask you a question. What do you have to lose? I don't have enough faith not to believe. If I am wrong, I haven't lost anything. If I am right, which I have no doubt that I am, I have eternal life with my God and Savior. All my debts have been paid in full. Either we can accept Jesus Christ's sacrifice as our payment for our sins, or we will have to pay the debt and sacrifice ourselves. We who have accepted Jesus Christ have been granted immunity from punishment not because of anything we have done but because of what he has done for us.

Again I ask you, what will you choose? Will you live empowered by the Spirit to be innocent or enslaved by the flesh to be guilty? The choice is yours. I pray after seeing the results of your choice, you will choose to be innocent. Your choice will have an earthly and eternal impact.

NOTES

1   Romans 8:1 NLT
2   Matthew 7:1 NLT
3   Luke 6:37 NLT
4   Proverbs: 21:2 NLT
5   Matthew 7:5 NLT
6   Romans 14:10–12 NLT
7   1 Corinthians 4:5 NLT
8   Romans 6:23 NLT
9   Psalm 103:12 NLT
10 1 Corinthians 2:9 NLT
11 John 12:48 NLT
12 2 Corinthians 5:10 NLT
13 Psalms 98:8–9 NLT
14 1 Peter 1:17 NLT
15 1 John 4:17 NLT
16 Revelation 22:12 NLT
17 2 Peter 3: 9 NLT
18 2 Peter 3:6–7 NLT
19 2 Thessalonians 1:7–8 NLT

CHAPTER 27

Life Vs Death

The next result of our choice to be in the Spirit or in the flesh is living in life versus living in death. Are you going to be empowered each day by the Spirit to live in life or enslaved by the flesh to live in death?

The Bible is clear about the way we are to live on earth.

If you cling to your life, you will lose it; but if you give up your life for me, you will find it.[1]

God wants us to give up our fleshly desires and to be empowered by the Holy Spirit.

The Spirit alone gives eternal life. Human effort accomplishes nothing. And the very words I have spoken to you are spirit and life.[2]

Jesus wants us to follow him rather than to lead a life of sin and attempted self-satisfaction. We know that our flesh cannot be satisfied. But by following Jesus, we can have a life of meaning, fulfillment, and purpose. Jesus knows what true life is all about and gave up his life for us to find it.

The power of the Spirit gives us life and not death. Jesus said:

I tell you the truth, those who listen to my message and believe in God who sent me have eternal life. They will never be condemned for their sins, but they have already passed from death into life. And I assure you that the time is coming, indeed it's here now, when the dead will hear my voice—the voice of the Son of God. And those who listen will live.[3]

At the moment you accepted Jesus Christ as your Savior, new life began in you. The dead to whom this verse refers are the spiritually dead and not the physically dead. Your flesh will die, but your spirit and soul will live during your time here on earth and eternally in the presence of God.

We are all on death row because we are all guilty of sinning against the law of God. But we have someone who has pleaded on our behalf. His plea was heard, the price was paid, and our verdict from the Judge of humanity is, "Not guilty. Debt paid in full."

So now there is no condemnation for those who belong to Christ Jesus. For the power of the life-giving Spirit has freed you through Christ Jesus from the power of sin that leads to death.[4]

Another verse says, "He is the one who has enabled us to represent his new covenant. This is a covenant, not of written laws, but of the Spirit. The old way ends in death; in the new way, the Holy Spirit gives life."[5] This verse says that trying to be saved by keeping the Old Testament laws will lead to death. No one but Jesus Christ has ever fulfilled the laws perfectly, so we are all condemned to death.

The law makes people realize their sins, but it can't give life. Under the new covenant, which means promise or agreement, eternal life comes from the Holy Spirit. The Spirit gives new life to all those who believe. The old laws (Ten Commandments) tell us how to live and obey God's commands, but they don't give us life. Life comes not from the rules of the Word of God but from a relationship with God.

And just to remind you again, "Rules without a relationship lead to rebellion."[6] So through a relationship with Jesus Christ, we have the ability to follow the rules when we are empowered by the Holy Spirit. With obedience come blessings and a life of satisfaction but not sacrifice.

Now that we have looked at some of the verses in the Bible that talk about life and death, let's compare the two. We only have two paths to follow in our earthly lives. One path is life and leads to heaven. The other path is death and leads to hell. Let's take a look at each one separately.

God created the path of life for each of us to follow. This path leads us to the purpose God created us to fulfill. It leads to a life filled with blessings, fulfillment, and hope in our eternal destination, which is heaven. Though our path here on earth is not always smooth, we know that we are not alone as we encounter bumps along the way. We will travel on the path through valleys and up mountaintops.

In the valleys of life, the soil is fertile and helps us to grow, mature, and to become more like Christ. To reach the mountaintops, we have to travel through the valleys, encountering detours and roadblocks that also help us grow, mature, and be more Christ-like. On the mountaintops, we celebrate our victories in life.

We are never alone on this path. Christ guides our steps with his light and his Word. On this path that leads to an eternal place with God, each bump, valley, detour, roadblock, and mountaintop leads us home. Praise God!

Here are some verses concerning the paths of life:

Seek his will in all you do, and he will show you which path to take.[7]

In all your ways submit to him, and he will make your paths straight.[8]

You make known to me the path of life; you will fill me with joy in your presence, with eternal pleasures at your right hand.[9]

The LORD makes firm the steps of the one who delights in him;[10]

Your word is a lamp to guide my feet and a light for my path.[11]

For I have stayed on God's paths; I have followed his ways and not turned aside.[12]

Now the other path—the Highway to Hell—leads to death. This is the wrong path and is headed in the wrong direction. God never intended for us to be on this path that leads to death and destruction. But through our own choices, we find that we are lost, and not only lost, but alone in the dark. When our flesh is in the driver's seat, we can't see where to go or how to get back on the right path.

On this path, there is no help. All are out for themselves. No one really cares enough to help anyone else find the way to the right path. There are no road signs to show us where to turn or to merge, and even if there were, we could not see them. With no light to see the way ahead, the route is full of wrecks. We face loneliness, insecurity, fear, anger, strife, bitterness, selfishness, burdens, regrets, pain, and so much more.

The eternal destination on this path is hell, and there is no way back. Once we reach hell, we are there forever and will be unimaginably miserable. Words cannot express the horrors that await at the end of this path, with no U-turns and only roadblocks.

But wait. If you are on this path of darkness, driven by your flesh, there is still hope. There is yet a way to connect to the path of light, and it is there for the taking. That way out has been there all along, but you just needed to stop and ask for directions.

The one who gives you the directions is Jesus Christ. He will give you a new direction and a new start on the path of light and life. He is your Savior and the one who saves you from reading the wrong map and taking the wrong direction. Now you have to do your part. You have to turn around. You have to turn from your sins and go a new direction in life. This turn is the most important one you will ever make in your life. It is not just a partial turn but a U-turn.

Our forgiveness is not limited by our sins, but by the extent to which we turn from them (repent). The Bible says, "Now repent of your sins and turn to God, so that your sins may be wiped away."[13] In Ezekiel, we read: "Put all your rebellion behind you, and find yourselves a new heart and a new spirit. For why should you die, O people of Israel? I don't want you to die, says the Sovereign Lord. Turn back and live!"[14]

We also have freedom from our slavery to sin and death while we are here on earth:

Therefore, dear brothers and sisters, you have no obligation to do what your sinful nature urges you to do. For if you live by its dictates, you will die. But if through the power of the Spirit you put to death the deeds of your sinful nature, you will live. For all who are led by the Spirit of God are children of God.[15]

Who is leading you? Is your driver your flesh or the Spirit? It is your choice to either follow your sinful desires and have death or to turn from your evil desires and have life here and for eternity. Choose life!

Now I ask you, which path are you going to follow? Unfortunately, more of us will follow the path that leads to death and destruction than the path that leads to life and satisfaction. For the Bible says, "You can enter God's Kingdom only through the narrow gate. The highway to hell is broad, and its gate is wide for the many who choose that way. But the gateway to life is very narrow and the road is difficult, and only a few ever find it."[16]

Are you going to go with the many or the few? I urge you to go with the few, for your decision has an eternal impact and a final destination with no U-turns. Turn now if you are going the wrong way before it is too late.

NOTES

1   Matthew 10:39 NLT
2   John 6:63 NLT
3   John 5:24–25 NLT
4   Romans 8:1–2 NLT
5   2 Corinthians 3:6 NLT
6   Andy Stanley, "Preaching The Grace of The Law," *Sermon Central*, November 29, 2010, https://www.sermoncentral.com/pastors-preaching-articles/andy-stanley-preaching-the-grace-of-the-law-763?ref=PreachingArticleDetails.
7   Proverbs 3:6 NLT
8   Proverbs 3:6 NIV
9   Psalm 16:11 NIV
10 Psalm 37:23 NIV
11 Psalm 119:105 NLT
12 Job 23:11 NLT
13 Acts 3:19 NLT
14 Ezekiel 18:30–32 NLT
15 Romans 8:12–14 NLT
16 Matthew 7:13–14 NLT

CHAPTER 28

Other Results

Now that we have discussed many results of our choices that we make to live each day empowered by the Spirit or by our flesh, I want to discuss a few other results that need to be mentioned.

The Earthly Trinity Vs the Holy Trinity

"We can serve one of two trinities in this life: the earthly trinity of me, myself, and I or the Holy Trinity of the Father, the Son, and the Holy Spirit." I heard our former pastor at First Baptist Church of Owasso, OK, Roger Ferguson, say this in one of his sermons. You cannot serve both. We are self-serving and self-sufficient or God-serving and God-sufficient. There is no middle ground.

When we live as if it is about *he* (Jesus Christ and not me) we really find what true life is all about. We have to die to self and live for Christ. When we live for ourselves, we make *me* the center of our world. We are not the center of the world, but God is. Everything was made by God and for God. He is the center of the world, and everything he created revolves around him. If we try to be the center of the universe, things don't work out for us. It is only when we accept that God is the center of the world and thus should be the center of our lives that we start to live in the center of his perfect will for our lives.

Seek the Kingdom of God above all else, and live righteously, and he will give you everything you need.[1]

Solid Rock Vs Sinking Sand

We can build our lives on the solid-rock foundation provided only by Jesus Christ, or we can live on our self-serving life, which is built on sinking sand.

Anyone who listens to my teaching and follows it is wise, like a person who builds a house on solid rock. Though the rain comes in torrents and the floodwaters rise and the winds beat against that house, it won't collapse because it is built on bedrock. But anyone who hears my teaching and doesn't obey it is foolish, like a person who builds a house on sand. When the rains and floods come and the winds beat against that house, it will collapse with a mighty crash.[2]

The higher you rise, the farther you can fall. The closer you are to the ground, the less distance you can fall and the less harm you can incur from a fall. It is harder to stumble and fall when you are on your knees, and it is impossible to fall when you are on your face—prostrate before the Lord. The security of the solid-rock foundation with a life built on Jesus Christ is the only place of earthly and eternal security.

Sanctification Vs Stagnation

We can choose to live empowered by the Spirit to be sanctified or enslaved by the flesh to be stagnant in our relationship with Christ. When we continue to grow up spiritually, we will know him more, love him more, please him more, and become more like Christ daily. As we grow closer to Christ and become like him, we make an invisible God increasingly more visible.

In Hebrews, we read about spiritual growth:

There is much more we would like to say about this, but it is difficult to explain, especially since you are spiritually dull and don't seem to listen. You have been believers so long now that you ought to be teaching others. Instead, you need someone to teach you again the basic things about God's word. You are like babies who need milk and cannot eat solid food. For someone who lives on milk is still an infant and doesn't know how to do what is right. Solid food is for those who are mature, who through training have the skill to recognize the difference between right and wrong.[3]

When you are passionate about something, you won't settle for the status quo. Doug Fields said this about the status quo: "Status quo appears easier. It doesn't take courage, risk, or passion. We become comfortable with our own small and selfish agendas and don't want to upset our apple carts. Status quo seems safe."[4]

In his letter to the Ephesians, Paul discussed the responsibility to grow spiritually and the results:

Now these are the gifts Christ gave to the church: the apostles, the prophets, the evangelists, and the pastors and teachers. Their responsibility is to equip God's people to do his work and build up the church, the body of Christ. This will continue until we all come to such unity in our faith and knowledge of God's Son that we will be mature in the Lord, measuring up to the full and complete standard of Christ.

Then we will no longer be immature like children. We won't be tossed and blown about by every wind of new teaching. We will not be influenced when people try to trick us with lies so clever they sound like the truth. Instead, we will speak the truth in love, growing in every way more and more like Christ, who is the head of his body, the church. He makes the whole body fit together perfectly. As each part does its own special work, it helps the other parts grow, so that the whole body is healthy and growing and full of love.[5]

We need to grow up spiritually by spending time with God through reading the Word of God (his love letter to us), praying, meditating on his Word, serving, fellowshipping with other believers, applying the Word of God to our lives, and becoming more obedient to his Word. As we do these things, we realize and recognize God more and more in our lives and become more like him.

So all of us who have had that veil removed can see and reflect the glory of the Lord. And the Lord—who is the Spirit—makes us more and more like him as we are changed into his glorious image.[6]

In turn, we can reveal Christ to others as we become more and more contagious in and for Christ. The contagious, Christ-like character we develop in our passionate pursuit of Christ infects others to want what we have. Infections are contagious regardless of whether people want to catch them or not. The closer we are to the infected, the more likely we will be infected.

Here's a story that illustrates spiritual growth. On their honeymoon in Turks and Caicos, my daughter and son-in-law went snorkeling—a first for my son-in-law. Enjoying the adventure, he turned to my daughter and said, "Hold my floaties; I am going deep!" I thought that was the funniest thing I had heard in a while, a good slogan for coffee mugs, cards, and T-shirts.

The statement also is a good fit for spiritual growth. We should tell our partners, friends, and those close to us, "Hold my floaties; I am going deep with God" as we dive into a deeper relationship with him. That is what deep spiritual maturity and sanctification are all about.

In our spiritual lives, we can choose to stay in shallow, stagnate water where things don't change and get filthier over time, or we can decide to grow and dive deep with God. When we stay in shallow waters, we have more potential to get caught up in the things or currents of the world. When we go deep with God, the more peaceful and beautiful our lives become.

Security Vs Insecurity

We can choose to be empowered by the Spirit to live in the true and unshakeable security of a life surrendered to Jesus Christ and built on a solid-rock foundation, or live with insecurity which results from a life built on our selfish, sin-filled flesh.

A few Bible verses about security that I want to share with you are below:

For the Lord is your security. He will keep your foot from being caught in a trap.[7]

Those who fear the Lord are secure; he will be a refuge for their children.[8]

Fear of the Lord leads to life, bringing security and protection from harm.[9]

Did you notice that these verses refer to the fear of the Lord as leading to security? This is because when we fear God, we respect his authority over our lives and surrender control to him.

Independent Vs Dependent

We can choose to live independently from the world and empowered by the Spirit or dependent on the world and enslaved by the flesh. When we live empowered by the spirit, we don't depend on the world to complete us. If we are not filled from within by the Holy Spirit, we are incomplete, and we will seek and depend on the external things of the world to complete us. When we are filled from within by the Holy Spirit, we are independent of the external things of the world (money, power, fame, sex, work, relationships, etc.) to complete us.

There is such beauty (natural beauty) in being independent of the things of the world because dependency on the things of the world results in ashes (fake beauty). Ashes come from fire, destruction, and death. But God can make beauty come from the ashes.

He will give a crown of beauty for ashes.[10]

The things of the world don't reach the depths of our soul and quench our thirst like the things of God can.

But those who drink the water I give will never be thirsty again. It becomes a fresh, bubbling spring within them, giving them eternal life.[11]

Jesus invites us to come to him and to receive the water (living water) that quenches our thirst from the things of the world and provides eternal life.

On the last day, the climax of the festival, Jesus stood and shouted to the crowds, "Anyone who is thirsty may come to me! Anyone who believes in me may come and drink! For the Scriptures declare, 'Rivers of living water will flow from his heart.' "[12]

The more dependent on God and empowered by the Spirit we are, the less dependent on the world and enslaved to the flesh we will be. When someone, like a child or animal, is completely dependent on us for survival, we have a special connection and bond with that someone. That is how God feels about those who are dependent on him to thrive, not just survive. God takes care of all our needs, not necessarily our wants.

Thankful Vs Unthankful

We can choose to live each day empowered by the Spirit to be thankful or enslaved by the flesh to be unthankful. When we accept the gift from God for the forgiveness of our sins because of the sinless sacrifice of his Son, Jesus Christ, we can't help but be thankful that we have gotten out of debt for free. Jesus paid it all.

Here is a Bible passage about thankfulness:

And let the peace that comes from Christ rule in your hearts. For as members of one body you are called to live in peace. And always be thankful. Let the message about Christ, in all its richness, fill your lives. Teach and counsel each other with all the wisdom he gives. Sing psalms and hymns and spiritual songs to God with thankful hearts.[13]

We are called to always live with thankful hearts. When we live with thankfulness, we are certainly different from the rest of the world.

Be thankful in all circumstances, for this is God's will for you who belong to Christ Jesus.[14]

This is a much bigger calling than just being thankful. When we are thankful in *all* circumstances, we really reveal our uniqueness in the world. You see, when bad things happen in our lives, we are still called to be thankful. How can we do that? We can trust God in all things and know that he has a plan for us through that hard time. We can do this by knowing that God is with us as we go through difficulties, and that he provides us with everything we need, including thankfulness.

One of my favorite verses in the Bible—my life verse for many years—is worth another mention: "And we know that in all things God works for the good of those who love him, who have been called according to his purpose."[15] Did you get that? All things work for our good—not some, but all. I am living proof of this verse that God works for the good of those who love God and live according to *his* purpose for their lives.

The world can't help but be unthankful because the world's promises offer what seems too good to be true, and they most always are just that. The world's promises are false, lies, deceptive, selfish, self-serving, and lead us down a path with no U-turns. The farther down this path we go, the harder it is to return.

Since the world offers you lies, how can you be thankful? You come up empty every time you buy into the lies of the world. The people of this world don't buy into your agenda of me, myself, and I because they are living in their own earthly trinity as well. All people who are living in the earthly trinity are out for themselves and have their own agendas. If we live in that way, it causes constant frustration and thanklessness. But the more thankful we are, the less unthankful we become.

The Promised Land Vs the Wilderness

We can choose to live each day in the promised land by being empowered by the Spirit or in the wilderness by being enslaved to the flesh. God took the Israelites out of Egypt but couldn't get Egypt out of them. Even after seeing many miracles from God, they still did not do what was pleasing to him. Because of their rebellion against God, only Joshua son of Nun, Caleb, and all the Israelites under the age of twenty years old were allowed to enter the Promised Land. The rest died because of their sins against God. Only an extremely small percentage of the Israelites were able to enter the land God had prepared for them.

This seems like a horrible situation the Israelites were in during their time on earth, but I would say that most of us Christians today are also living in the wilderness instead of the promised land that God has for his children. That promised land includes living with passion for him and living empowered by the Spirit. When we live this way, we enjoy all the benefits listed in this book and many more.

If we would live filled up and overflowing with the Spirit, we would be so different that others couldn't help but notice and want what we have. When God is part of every fiber of our being, we infect others for Christ everywhere we go.

If this isn't happening in and through our lives, the cause is our lack of living empowered by the Spirit. Most of us still live in a default, flesh-driven mode, wandering in the desert with the rest of the world. We might be saved from death but not saved from self.

Thus, my burden to write this book was to help others live in the promised land that God has for each of his children. We just have to do our part by obeying, growing in our relationship with Jesus Christ, surrendering all control to him, serving, trusting, and watching God move us to a beautiful and satisfying place in the promised land, which is overflowing with the Holy Spirit.

We can choose to wander in the wilderness like most Christians or to partake in the goodness of the promised land that God has for his children here on earth. When we live in the promised land, we are in the very center of God's perfect will for our lives. When we are in the center of God's perfect will for our lives, other believers and nonbelievers will notice.

Eternal Vs Earthly

We can choose to live each day empowered by the Spirit to keep our eyes on eternal things or enslaved by the flesh to keep our eyes on earthly things. We need to change our focus from earthly to eternal things.

Since you have been raised to new life with Christ, set your sights on the realities of heaven, where Christ sits in the place of honor at God's right hand. Think about the things of heaven, not the things of earth.[16]

When we do this, we take the things here on earth much more lightly. When we know that earth is not our home and our time here is short, we will live life with a different mind-set. We live a much more joy-filled life when we change our focus from an earthly to an eternal mind-set—one that is out of this world!

Transparent Vs Opaque

We can choose to live each day empowered by the Spirit to be transparent or enslaved by the flesh to be opaque. When we live transparently, we create common ground and a level playing field for all to approach us.

Living transparently means that we admit and share all the mistakes we have made in our lives so that others can learn from them. In their quest to learn from those mistakes, we can share how Jesus Christ made it possible for us to admit and learn from our mistakes.

During the more than ten years that I have taught students—mostly high school girls—in Sunday school at my local church, I have attributed my spiritual impact in their lives more to my transparency than anything else I may have done or said to them.

Transparency is living from the inside out. It is making the invisible parts of our lives visible for others to see. In doing this, we make God and the spiritual transformation he has done inside us more visible.

All Vs None

We can live with all or none of these results of the choices we make in our lives. No, we can't have some of them and not others. We are either living in the presence of God through Jesus Christ or in the absence of God by sinning against him. We either have access to all or none of these results. *Please get this.*

Now let me go a little further with this concept. We can have more or less of these results in our lives. The more we grow in our relationship with Christ, the more we will experience the spiritual and positive results of our choices; the less we grow in our relationship with Christ, the less we will experience the spiritual and positive results of our choices. The options we have because of the choices in our lives will result in having more or less of all the benefits or none at all. You can't have more or less of nothing, because there is none to start with.

If we are working towards sanctification instead of stagnation in our walk with Christ, we will experience all and more of the benefits mentioned in this book in our lives. These benefits to living a life that is pleasing to God and the results of our choices are priceless, and everyone ultimately is relentlessly pursuing all of them. When you live in the presence of God, experiencing all the benefits mentioned in this book, and getting more and more of them as you are sanctified, you are filled up and overflowing with the Holy Spirit. Living this way is being in the earthly Promised Land that most of the Israelites never entered because of the bad choices they had made in their lives. This is also true of Christians today; most of us are not living life to the fullest and overflowing from the Holy Spirit, the life that is available and free to all of us.

NOTES

1   Matthew 6:33 NLT

2   Matthew 7:24–27 NLT

3   Hebrews 5:11–14 NLT

4   Doug Fields, "HomeWord Daily Devotionals," *Status Quo*, July 18, 2018, https://www.crosswalk.com/devotionals/homeword/status-quo-homeword-july-18-2018.html.

5   Ephesians 4:11–16 NLT

6   2 Corinthians 3:18 NLT

7   Proverbs 3:26 NLT

8   Proverbs 14:26 NLT

9   Proverbs 19:23 NLT

10 Isaiah 61:3 NLT

11 John 4:14 NLT

12 John 7:37 and 38 NLT

13 Colossians 3:15 and 16 NLT

14 1 Thessalonians 5:18 NLT

15 Romans 8:28 NIV

16 Colossians 3:1 and 2 NLT

PART THREE

WINNING THE BATTLE

CHAPTER 29

Victory Vs Defeat

We can choose to live each day empowered by the Spirit to be victorious or enslaved by the flesh to be defeated. Living victoriously as the Spirit overpowers our flesh is the ultimate goal for us as Christians. Let's look at what we need to do to live victoriously in the spiritual battles that are a constant threat in and through our lives. There are several things we have to do in order to live in victory over the constant spiritual battle between our Spirit and flesh.

1. If you haven't accepted God as your personal Lord and Savior through God's Son, Jesus Christ, then this is your first step. The Bible says, "If you openly declare that Jesus is Lord and believe in your heart that God raised him from the dead, you will be saved."[1]

2. Confess your sins to God. If you are in a repetitive, habitual sin pattern, repent (turn and go the other way) and return to God. Scripture says, "But if we confess our sins to him, he is faithful and just to forgive us our sins and to cleanse us from all wickedness."[2]

3. Spend quiet time with God daily by reading the Word of God (the Bible), praying, journaling, meditating on the Word of God and applying his Word to your life. This helps you grow in your relationship with him.

4. Obey his Word. When we are obedient to God and what his Word says about how we should live, great blessings and spiritual growth come from this obedience. Through our obedience to God, we apply God's principles and commands in our lives. The Bible tells us, "You must love the Lord your God and always obey his requirements, decrees, regulations, and commands."[3]

5. Serving God with the spiritual gifts we have been given will grow your relationship with God to a new deeper level. When we are fulfilling the purpose that he created us to do within the body of Christ, there is a fulfillment that is beyond description.

In addition to these steps, the other key to victory is the word *all*. Let me give you a few verses to describe what I mean. One of the two greatest commandments in the Bible is "Love the Lord your God with all your heart and with all your soul and with all your mind and with all your strength."[4] Did you catch the word *all*? God wants all and not just part of us.

We, as Christians, seem to compartmentalize God in our lives. For example, he can have our time on Sunday mornings, but we do what we want to do with the rest of our time. The same is true for our money. God can have the leftovers, but not the first of our earnings.

If you want to know how much of your *all* God has, look at your calendar and your bank account—on your phone, of course. Time, money, and the use of technology occupy a large part of our lives. These places are where we can give him all or just a part of ourselves. When we truly comprehend what God has done for us, we will be able to give him all our lives.

God needs to infiltrate every fiber of our being. That is when he has all of our heart, mind, soul, and strength.

This next verse tells us how our all is equally critical in attaining victory in our lives during the constant spiritual battle we face: "You will seek me and find me when you seek me with all your heart."[5] So again, we see the word *all*. We will find God only when we seek him with all of our heart.

God Does HIS Part by Revealing Himself to Us When we Seek HIM With ALL of Our Heart. Our Part is to Recognize it as God and Give HIM the Glory.

I am living proof of this fact in my spiritual walk with God. During the infant and toddler phases of my relationship with God, I started noticing him in the little and big things of my life. When I would recognize him and give him the glory, he revealed himself more to me. God does more than his part in our relationship with him.

Besides loving and seeking God with our all, the other thing we need to do to win the battle is to put on our spiritual armor.

A final word: Be strong in the Lord and in his mighty power. Put on all of God's armor so that you will be able to stand firm against all strategies of the devil. For we are not fighting against flesh-and-blood enemies, but against evil rulers and authorities of the unseen world, against mighty powers in this dark world, and against evil spirits in the heavenly places.

Therefore, put on every piece of God's armor so you will be able to resist the enemy in the time of evil. Then after the battle you will still be standing firm. Stand your ground, putting on the belt of truth and the body armor of God's righteousness. For shoes, put on the peace that comes from the Good News so that you will be fully prepared. In addition to all of these, hold up the shield of faith to stop the fiery arrows of the devil. Put on salvation as your helmet, and take the sword of the Spirit, which is the word of God."[6]

Spiritual armor is crucial in being victorious in our spiritual battles. All the pieces of armor except for the sword are weapons of defense. The only piece of the armor that is offensive is the sword of the Spirit, which is the Word of God. We need to put on this spiritual armor daily to protect ourselves from the devil and his fallen angels, who are hard at work, trying to trip us up in our walk with God.

Be alert and of sober mind. Your enemy the devil prowls around like a roaring lion looking for someone to devour.[7]

Note that this verse specifically speaks about the devil, our enemy, who is looking for someone to devour. We need to be alert (aware of this constant threat and battle) and of a sober mind. We should be careful not to be mentally impaired by alcohol or drugs of any kind so that we can think clearly and recognize when we are being attacked. I can say that most of the mistakes I have made in my life happened when I was mentally impaired through the use of alcohol and/or drugs.

The last thing I want to discuss in our effort to live victoriously is to pray constantly.

Pray in the Spirit at all times and on every occasion. Stay alert and be persistent in your prayers for all believers everywhere.[8]

We are all under attack, and it takes us all praying for each other to help us win the battle.

For every child of God defeats this evil world, and we achieve this victory through our faith. And who can win this battle against the world? Only those who believe that Jesus is the Son of God.[9]

One evening, my daughter and I had gone out to eat, which wasn't uncommon in our home while she was growing up. When we left the restaurant, there was a huge line to get into the restaurant. When we got to the car, I started talking to her about God's favor and how he always provides for his children.

As we traveled down the road on our ten-minute drive home, a little dog ran out in front of us. I hit it, and it rolled under our car. We immediately pulled over and stopped, along with several other cars. The dog crossed the other lane of the road and laid down in the ditch. We approached her, but she got up and started walking the opposite way from the direction we had been traveling. Shocked and thankful that the dog could walk, we followed as she went down a driveway to a specific house.

As soon as she approached the house, a car pulled into the driveway and a young man got out and shouted, "Lilly!" The dog immediately turned and walked toward the man, who was obviously her owner.

In the meantime, another car had stopped in front of the house, and the driver got out and said, "I am a veterinarian and saw what happened." He assessed Lilly to be in fine condition. The owner agreed that she was acting normal. We all were relieved and elated that the dog apparently had not suffered any injuries from the accident.

Needless to say, my daughter and I both recognized God in that moment. He not only had the owner show up, but also a veterinarian. We were in awe of God and his favor and provision during this divine moment in our lives. That is just one of many more stories I could relate about how God has shown up in my life.

Immediately after I was delivered from myself and my slavery to sin, God became part of every fiber of my inner being. Since then, God has been a part of every decision I have made in my life and a part of most conversations. I constantly mention him and recognize him in my life. How could my daughter not notice and imitate me?

You see, if we compartmentalize God, our children will too. **Children are Sponges, and They will Absorb Whatever we Pour in Their Lives.** What kind of life do you want your children to lead? What kind of spiritual legacy are you going to give them? If we truly love our children, we will invest in their spirituality more than any other aspect of their lives. We can't live a fulfilled life without God and don't want our children to have a life without him either.

So, let me ask you this, are you a fair-weather follower, a foul-weather follower, or a faithful-weather follower? Let me explain the difference so you can accurately answer this question.

Fair-weather followers follow God during the good times, but when the bad times come, they run from and not toward him. Foul-weather followers call out to God in the bad times, but ignore him during the good times. Faithful-weather followers are all in and follow God regardless of the weather. This is the kind of children God wants us to be.

In order to be victorious in the spiritual battle that we constantly face in our lives between the spirit and the flesh, we have to give God our all. When we rely on him totally, he gives us the power through his Holy Spirit to live in a way where our flesh is only the covering for his spirit, which overflows in and through us.

Others won't have to look very hard to see the overflow in our lives. This saturated sponge spills out more and more of the Holy Spirit which infiltrates others around us. This is what a life of victory during our spiritual battles really looks like. When we live this way, many lives will be impacted for the kingdom of God.

NOTES

1   Romans 10:9 NLT
2   1 John 1:9 NLT
3   Deuteronomy 11:1 NLT
4   Mark 12:30 NIV
5   Jeremiah 29:13 NIV
6   Ephesians 6: 10–17 NLT
7   1 Peter 5:8 NIV
8   Ephesians 6:18 NLT
9   1 John 5:4 and 5 NLT

CHAPTER 30

The Benefits of Victory

Let's discuss all the benefits of victory that have been mentioned in detail in the prior chapters of this book. We get the fruits of the Spirit, which are love, joy, peace, patience, kindness, righteousness, gentleness, faithfulness, and self-control. The other results of our choice to live in the presence of God through Jesus Christ are humility, purity, satisfaction, rest, freedom, light, hope, connection, being found, newness, bravery, strength, generosity, innocence, life, the Holy Trinity, solid rock foundation, sanctification, security, independence, thankfulness, the promised land, eternity, transparency, and all.

When you look at all of these priceless attributes of living a life empowered by the Holy Spirit and not enslaved by the flesh, isn't this what we really desire in our lives? I will answer that question from my personal experience. Yes! Since I met the Lord by asking Jesus Christ into my life, I have learned how to live more and more victoriously. In this pursuit of victory, my life has been filled up and is overflowing with the love of God, the fruits of the Spirit, and the results of my choices that I have listed above.

In my victorious life, I have become deeply burdened as I have seen that most Christians are still living in defeat. The reason God put the message of this book on my heart was to share it with others in hopes of helping them become more victorious in their relationships with Christ.

If we can get this book's message from God into our heads, and more importantly, into our hearts, we will live much more fulfilling, purpose-driven lives, and we will become more effective in impacting the kingdom of God.

Ultimately, our primary goal in our spirit-filled lives while we are here on earth should be to impact the kingdom of God. The way we can have the most impact in the kingdom of God is to live and look differently than the world does. When we live filled with the fruits of the Spirit and other positive attributes that we receive when we live in the presence of God, we will be noticed and contagious in our influence toward others—believers and nonbelievers alike.

As I continue to strive to overcome the spiritual battles in my life, God gives me what I need to live in victory. This life of living more in victory than in defeat is a blessed one that I could never have imagined until I tasted it personally. Now that I have tasted what victory is like, I want to share it with others so they can taste it too. This victorious life will be rewarded temporarily on earth (because this is not our home) and eternally in heaven at a much greater magnitude than we could ever imagine. This type of eternal victory never fades, never devalues, is never beaten, and is never forgotten like our earthly victories. These victories can be enjoyed now and eternally.

CHAPTER 31

Our Earthly Purpose

We were all created to be a part of God's plan for the world. In God's plan, we each fulfill a specific purpose that we are given by God to impact others for the kingdom of God.

In Jeremiah, we read, " 'For I know the plans I have for you,' says the Lord. 'They are plans for good and not for disaster, to give you a future and a hope.' "[1]

We have a choice. We can choose to live according to the purpose we were created for or not. When we are living according to our purpose, that is when we really find true life. When I teach my high school girls about God, I experience a euphoria that is better than anything the world could offer. There are no hangovers or regrets. I do know that I am doing exactly what God created me to do—living right in the center of God's perfect will, plan, and purpose for my life. There is no better and more secure place to be.

When we are living according to the purpose he created us to do, we are part of God's plan for the world. God's plan will be done with or without us.

You can make many plans, but the Lord's purpose will prevail.[2]

God's plan will be successful, and he will win the ultimate victory in the end. We know the end of the story. Revelations 20 says:

And I saw a great white throne and the one sitting on it. The earth and sky fled from his presence, but they found no place to hide. I saw the dead, both great and small, standing before God's throne. And the books were opened, including the Book of Life. And the dead were judged according to what they had done, as recorded in the books. The sea gave up its dead, and death and the grave gave up their dead. And all were judged according to their deeds. Then death and the grave were thrown into the lake of fire. This lake of fire is the second death. And anyone whose name was not found recorded in the Book of Life was thrown into the lake of fire.[3]

We know who wins the battle in the end. Don't you want to be part of the winning team?

When my flesh dies and my spirit meets God face-to-face, I want him to say to me, "Well done my good and faithful servant."[4] I want to tell him, "It is finished"[5] like Jesus did before he died on the cross. I want to know that I have finished the purpose that he created me to fulfill.

I pray that the message in this book will give you the tools you need to live in victory over the constant battle between your spirit and your flesh. In doing so, you will fulfill the purpose he created you to do, and you will also be able to say, "It is finished" when you meet God. Praise God!

NOTES

1   Jeremiah 29:11 NLT
2   Proverbs 19:21 NLT
3   Revelations 20:11–15 NLT
4   Matthew 25:21 NLT
5   John 19:30 NLT

CONCLUSION

It is my burden, prayer, and the deepest desire of my heart that this book will be a wake-up call to Christians around the world about how they need to live and to look different from the world. I pray this book is not just a message but a movement for all Christians to start being victorious in the constant battle between our spirits and our flesh. I pray that the Holy Spirit provides each of you with an increasing amount of fruit and other spiritual attributes as you grow in your relationship with God.

We, as Christians, who are continuing to grow in our relationship with God, can become more like Christ and less like the world. In becoming more like Christ, we look different and can be contagious in our influence of others by helping them to win their own battle between their spirits and their flesh. Are you ALL IN?!